Around The Table

A Culinary Memoir by Two Sisters

Around The Table

A Culinary Memoir by Two Sisters

Michele Castellano Senac
& Lorrie Castellano

Copyright ©2013 Michele Castellano Senac and Lorrie Castellano

Copyright ©2013 Photography by Michele Castellano Senac and Lorrie Castellano

ALL RIGHTS RESERVED. No part of this book may be reproduced without written permission from the publisher, except in the case of brief excerpts in critical reviews and articles. Address all inquiries to: There Are Diamonds in the Sky, ThereAreDiamondsInTheSky.com

ISBN-13: 978-1493732456

ISBN-10: 1493732455

First Edition

Published in the United States of America
ThereAreDiamondsInTheSky.com

Cover photograph by Lorrie Castellano

Design by Kay Turnbaugh

Dedicated to our grandparents and parents

And as a gift to our children and grandchildren

Contents

Introduction   xiii

PART ONE
The Story of Our Family
La Storia della nostra Famiglia
by Lorrie Castellano

1 The Cibella Family   3

   Caposele, Italy, and Newark, New Jersey   4
   Tomaso Cibella and Camille Salvatoriello Cibella   8
      Their children:
      Rose Cibella   9
      Mary Cibella Stefanelli   16
      Angelina "Angie" Cibella Aulise   19
      Loretta "Cleo" Cibella Castellano   56
      Eleanore Cibella Hockin   22

2 The Castellano Family   31

   Newark, New Jersey   32
   Michael Angelo Castellano, Sr. and Philomena Ilaria Castellano   33
      Their children:
      Nicholas Ilaria Castellano   40
      Philomena "Mena" Volpe Castellano Fried   44
      Michael Angelo Castellano, Jr.   46
      Joseph John Castellano   72
      Josephine "Dolly" Castellano Vuocolo   49

3 The Uniting of Both Families: Our Parents   55

   Joseph John Castellano and Loretta Cibella Castellano   56
   LaFest' – Caposele, Italy and Newark, New Jersey   78

PART TWO

Recipes and Stories Around the Table

Ricette e Racconti Intorno al Tavolo

by Michele Castellano Senac

4 Small Bites - Piccoli Morsi — 85

- Cannellini Bean Bruschetta — 86
- Sweet/Sour Cherry Peppers — 87
- Stuffed Hot Cherry Peppers — 89
- Stuffed Mushrooms — 90
- Antipasto — 93
- Roasted Peppers — 94
- Stuffed Artichokes — 97
- Fennel and Olives — 99
- Rice Balls — 100
- Taralles — 101
- Mozzarella and Tomato – Caprese — 103
- A Word About Olive Oil — 104

5 Tomato Sauce ("Gravy") with Meat – *Salsa di Pomodoro e Carni* — 105

- A Word About Tomatoes — 107
- Tomato Sauce and Meatballs, Braciole and Sausage — 106
- Tomato Sauce with Sausage — 111
- Marinara – Meatless Sauce — 113
- Quick Fresh Tomato Sauce — 114
- Making Italian Sausage — 115

6 Pasta — 119

A Word About Pasta	120
Linguini and Clams	122
Spaghetti Aglio e olio	124
Cavatelli	126
Pastina with the Egg	129
Peas and Pasta	130
Fusilli, Ziti or Cavatelli with Broccoli or Cauliflower	132
Pasta e Fagioli	135
Cecida and Pasta	137
Pasta Puttanesca	138
Bows with Pot Cheese	140
Lasagna	142
Ravioli	144

7 Salads – *Insalata* — 147

Leafy Greens	149
Italian Salad Dressing	149
Broccoli Rabe Salad	151
Broccoli Salad	152
Potato Salad	154
Tomato Salad	156
Fennel and Olives	99
Christmas Day Orange & Olive Salad	158

8 Pizza — 159

Tomato and Cheese Pizza

Mom's Pizza	160
Lorrie's Pizza	164
Anchovy Pizza	202

9 Canning Tomatoes — 167

- Mom's Canned Tomatoes — 171
- Lorrie's Canned Tomatoes — 171

10 Everyday Meals – *i Pasta di Tutti i Giorni* — 175

- Polenta with Marinara Sauce — 176
- Lentil Soup — 177
- Eggplant Parmigiana — 179
- Menest' and Beans (Escarole and Beans) — 180
- Jambought' — 183
- Spinach and Potatoes — 184
- String Beans and Potatoes — 185
- Peppers and Eggs — 186
- Sausage and Peppers — 189
- Settlement House Meatloaf — 190
- Chicken and Potatoes — 193
- Veal Cutlets — 194
- Peas and Pasta — 130
- Fusilli, Ziti or Cavatelli with Broccoli or Cauliflower — 132
- Pasta e Fagioli — 135
- Cecida and Pasta — 137

11 Christmas Eve - Feast of the Seven Fishes – *Natale Festa Vigilia dei Sette Pesci* — 197

- Menu — 201
- Antipasto — 93
- Tomato and Cheese Pizza — 160
- Anchovy Pizza — 202
- Stuffed Mushrooms — 90
- Stuffed Hot Cherry Peppers — 89

Stuffed Artichokes	97
Cappellini and Anchovies	204
Baccala – Salted Cod Fish	206
Scungelli Salad – Conch	208
Shrimp Scampi	210
Shrimp & Roasted Peppers	212
Fried Smelts	214
Broccoli Salad	152
Fennel and Olive Salad	99

12 Sweets – *Dolci* — 215

Sesame Cookies	217
Pound Cake	219
Coffee Cake	220
Thumbprint Butter Cookies	221
Cream Puffs	222
Italian Cream Cake	224
Bowknots	226
Struffoli	228
Knots – Italian Wedding Cookies	231
Pizzelle	233

13 Putting It All Together — 235

Acknowledgments	240
About the Authors	241
Index	242

Introduction

Some of our most vivid memories from childhood come from sitting around the tables of our parents, grandparents and aunts. The kitchen is the center of Italian-American life, and the table is the gathering place. The table has always been an anchor for our family. Every night growing up, the kitchen table was set and the family gathered for a meal. It was there we felt the security of being together, exchanging experiences, catching up on family gossip, and discussing topics ranging from school to politics. Many weekend nights our parents sat at the dining room table with family and friends for hours, drinking demitasse or a cordial, and catching up on their lives. Our holidays were always spent around the dining room table. Today, these traditions continue in our homes and in our children's homes, with the table supporting a great meal, simple or elaborate, and always filled with lively conversation.

As in any memoir, our memories are subjective and influenced by personal emotions. Though others may remember events and details differently, the intention was to capture the essence of our family life.

Michele's writing about the family recipes and memories would not have told the complete story without Lorrie's account of the family history. The courage and experiences of our grandparents, parents and extended family had such a great influence on us and were an inspiration to us in writing this culinary memoir.

—Michele Castellano Senac and Lorrie Castellano

Premiare

Part One

The Story of Our Family
La Storia della nostra Famiglia

Front row, left to right: Aunt Eleanore, Mom, Cousin Mary Ann, Dad. Second row: Grandma and Grandpa Castellano, Grandpa and Grandma Cibella, circa 1938

Grandma and Grandpa Cibella, 1949

Chapter 1

The Cibella Family

Tomaso Cibella
(6/7/1879 to 6/7/1976)

Camille Salvatoriello Cibella
(11/23/1879 to 5/6/1954)

Their children:

Rose Cibella
(11/10/1904 to 4/8/1995)

Mary Cibella Stefanelli
(12/7/1906 to 11/8/1997)

Angelina "Angie" Cibella Aulisi
(5/5/1909 to 12/11/2003)

Loretta "Cleo" Cibella Castellano
(4/19/1915 to 1/18/2011)

Eleanore Cibella Hockin
(12/14/1920)

Caposele, Italy (1999)

The rain was pouring down when we left Sorrento in search of Caposele, a tiny mountain town in south central Italy. I had a name, Gerard Guarino, a nephew of my maternal grandfather. That would make him my second cousin. I had an address, but no one had answered letters to this address since the earthquake in 1980. I wasn't sure my second cousin was still around to be found. I'd been told Caposele was too small to be on the map, but when I checked it was there. I'd heard the name over and over throughout my childhood. Old friends of my grandparents who'd stop by for coffee were always from Caposele. Aunt Rose regularly wrote to our relatives in that hamlet of Avellino Province. St. Gerard not only had a feast in the streets of Newark, but was the patron saint of Caposele. My mother often told me my grandparents were married in a little church there and that a registry existed in which the marriage was recorded. Of course, I wanted to see Caposele.

My husband, Roger Fisher, who is from Manchester, England, was skeptical.

"You mean we're going to see people you've never met, who don't know you, and most of all don't even know you're coming?"

None of that bothered me. I had no doubt that a warm welcome awaited us. Italians are known for their inclination to make anyone who's willing into a relative and then greet them as long lost. What worried me was the language. I didn't speak Italian, and I was sure they didn't speak English. I foresaw a lot of awkward silences and embarrassed smiles. But even with my husband's misgivings and my ambivalence, we drove on through the heavy rain, making sure we were on A3 and didn't miss the Contursi Terme exit to 91. From there it just took some faith that signs would lead us to an even smaller road and eventually Caposele.

It was still raining when we took the last curve into Caposele. There it was, a small mountain hamlet built on a hill. The houses were white stucco and obviously had been rebuilt after the earthquake 15 years before. I felt a thrill to see for the first time my grandparents' home town, a town they left in 1903.

With Aunt Rose's surely outdated address, a camera, and an Italian dictionary, Roger and I parked the car, braved the rain and began looking for Via Garibaldi, 13. Obvious outsiders, we drew curious stares from the few people who were out walking. When we found the street, there was no number 13. I must admit I felt some relief.

Gerardo and Josephina in Caposele

Roger and I headed back to the car feeling that we were spared the forced smiles and embarrassed silences, but we could at least say we had tried.

The rain let up so we decided to take a walk to see the sights of the town. We were on a typical Caposele street, cobblestoned and narrow. I was thinking about my grandfather and grandmother. When they were young, they left this town with a dream of starting a whole new life in a place called Newark, New Jersey, in America. Southern Italy was poor back then. This little mountain town didn't hold much of a future for them. What courage it must have taken to leave all that was familiar and board a ship to a place so far away – to leave their family and friends and not know if they'd ever see them again. And I thought it was because of their bravery that I became who I am today. I wondered what kind of life I would have had if they hadn't made that enormous trip.

My thoughts were interrupted by the beep of a truck backing up on the narrow street. The sidewalk was non-existent, and when an infrequent car came by pedestrians ducked into the nearest doorway for safety. We did the same, and as our eyes adjusted to the light, I saw two little old ladies dressed completely in black from head to toe. They were short and round. Silver hair, parted in the middle, was all you could see under their black head shawls. They were so much like characters in a Fellini film that I almost looked around for the cameras.

Josephina in her garden

"Sono Americana?" one of the women asked. "Sì." Smile. Deep Breath. "La mia nonno essi sono da Caposele." "Come si chiamano?" I told them my cousin's name, and they became very excited, talking so fast I could only get a few words. Something about a hairdresser and closed on Mondays. Finally I understood. He is not a hairdresser but one of his daughters is. Their hand movements indicated the salon was somewhere to the right, seemingly, in the mountains. What happened next was unexpected. One of the women flagged down the next car, spoke rapidly to the driver and literally pushed us into the back seat. She reassured us that we were in good hands by telling us that the couple knew English because their daughter lived in Los Angeles. Our weak protests were waved aside with a "va bene." From the back seat of the car I could see the satisfied smiles of our two foreign film guides. Job well done. This would be talked about for many days.

Knowing the Italian penchant for making wild assumptions and saying them loud enough so they sound true, it became rapidly evident that this couple did not speak English, even with having a daughter in Los Angeles. Roger had the dictionary, and I had the phrase book. Our hands were working overtime, flipping pages. Roger and I looked at each other. What next? Anything was possible. We shrugged and hoped for the best.

It seemed like an eternity, but only five minutes later we were in front of the hair salon and, as our original guides had said, it was closed. Today was Monday. This did not deter our driver. They consulted the many neighbors who opened doors, pulled back curtains and stopped on the street to stare. As I climbed out of the car, I looked at the building across the street and there, on the second floor, were two women looking out their windows exactly as I remember Italian women doing in Newark when I was a girl. I thought the gossip tonight around their dinner tables would be good.

Rushing behind the shop, our hijacked driver finally produced a couple who looked puzzled. They were in their 60s. My cousin, Gerardo, was a bit reluctant with a skeptical look on his face. His wife, Josephina, was eager for this adventure. She was a heavyset woman who wore a large apron over her printed dress. Her hair was pulled back in a bun. Gerardo was slim and short. He wore a cap and, to my surprise, looked just like my grandfather. I couldn't help smiling. By this time, a small crowd had gathered around us, and I began my speech in Italian: "Sono nipote di Tomaso Cibella." With the name of my grandfather, Gerardo's face lit up. He opened his arms, and we hugged. "Mia marito, Roger," was all I said and we were family. They invited us to their home where a fire burned in the kitchen hearth and, true to Italian hospitality, food began to appear. Roger and I smiled at each other. This was going to be fine.

The kitchen fire burned directly on the tiled floor. We sat around it on tiny children's chairs to get the direct heat. The room across the courtyard held the wood-burning oven where Josephina baked bread every day and taralles, a fennel flavored circle of dough hardened in the oven. Taralles have always been my favorite. Whenever I'm in Newark I stop by the same bakery that has been making them since I was a child. My aunts would send care packages to me when I moved to California, and taralles would always be included. Josephina showed me the olives she cures herself, her brick oven, vegetable garden and grape vines. She spread the table with homemade sausage, cheeses, homegrown grapes, olives, roasted peppers and delicious freshly baked bread. Her kitchen was hung with garlic, onion and peppers drying for the winter. Her herb garden was just outside the kitchen door. We talked simply, translating the main words so that we could fill in the blanks and guess at the general direction of the conversation. We smiled a lot, as I suspected we would. We were family. I'd found the place where my grandparents were born, and I'd found the family they'd left behind.

Life in America

Grandma and Grandpa Cibella, 1949

The life of an immigrant at the turn of the century was hard. Tomaso Cibella entered Ellis Island in February, 1903. Camille Salvatoriello, his wife, followed five months later. The plan was not to consummate their marriage until they were in America. Neither wanted to take the chance of Camille traveling for a month in the hold of a ship while pregnant. It was a good plan. And it was how they lived their lives in America: well thought out, one step at a time. Camille gave birth eight times; five babies survived. Their first child, Rose, was born November 10, 1904; Mary was born December 11, 1906; Angelina, known as Angie, arrived on May 5, 1909; Loretta Columbia, my mom, known as Cleo, was born April 19, 1915; and finally, Eleanore, on December 14, 1920.

If you look at a map of Newark, the places Tomaso and Camille lived were all in the same neighborhood: 14 and 197 Garside Street, 85 Mount Prospect Avenue, Lake Street, and 308 Clifton Avenue. They were all located next to Branch Brook Park in what was known as the First Ward, the Italian section of town, Little Italy of Newark, New Jersey. Branch Brook Park was a perfect harvesting ground for Camille's greens. I'd see her bent over, her cloth bag over her arm, picking dandelions and various edible greens from the lawns of Branch Brook Park. It embarrassed me at the time to see my grandma gathering her food from a public park. But it didn't stop me from eating them. I loved her minest' and beans, as she called it. The correct word is minestre, but true to the dialect, the ending is dropped. Those greens cooked in olive oil and garlic with some cannellini beans could not be beat. The recipe as told to me by Aunt Rose includes how to deal with the sand. That's Branch Brook Park sand! Tomaso and Camille Cibella were hard working, resourceful, focused people in spite of or maybe because of the challenges they faced as immigrants.

Rose Cibella (11/10/1904–4/8/1995)

I walked up the concrete path to Aunt Rose's apartment house, a nondescript blocky building constructed under the ill-advised urban renewal that Newark undertook in the 1970s. Little Italy was torn down, and these plain concrete buildings took its place. The only redeeming quality of this building was the dark green awning over the glass front door. It was a far cry from the lovely three-story house at 308 Clifton Avenue where most of my memories resided. Disappointment and a sense of loss overtook me as I stepped into the dimly lit entrance. The building itself was clean and sparse, well cared for, but still it lacked the warmth that I'd always felt when entering the Cibella home. I was filled with remorse that I'd been away so long, as if my presence could have prevented these changes, including my aunt getting older. I was in town to attend her 90th birthday party the following day and had been in California for the last 29 years. Our visits during those years were regretfully few. I took the elevator to the fifth floor and stepped out into a long narrow hallway sealed from natural light. Monotonous doors lined each side of the hall. The memories of those Sundays spent with my family at 308 Clifton Avenue made the cold, indifferent hall all the more bleak. I found number 505 and knocked. Aunt Rose was there in an instant as though she were waiting right behind the door. When she opened it, there it all was. The same heavy dark wood furniture, her tatted doilies right where they'd always been, and the smells from the small galley kitchen took me instantly back to Clifton Avenue. My memories unpacked their bags and moved into this tiny apartment.

The house smelled of olive oil, garlic and escarole. My aunt had made my favorite dish: escarole and beans or as she, like her mother, called it minest' and beans. The table was already set, and on it were thick slices of Italian bread, roasted peppers and a small plate of eggplant parmesan. As usual, a small glass of red wine was at my place, in a glass that could have been my grandfather's. I remember him saying, "Drink. Wine is good for your blood." And apparently it was because he lived to be 96 and in good health.

"You have to get all the sand out," she said when I asked her to teach me how to make minest' and beans. I smiled, remembering my grandma's bent figure in Branch Brook Park.

Aunt Rose had shrunk. I remember her as tall and straight. Now she was shorter and frail, but she still had that air of complete control. Her hair was pure white and soft around her face. Her mouth turned down slightly at the corners so she looked like a disapproving teacher about to tell me to throw back my shoulders, pull in my stomach and don't shuffle when I walk. Just looking at her made me stand up straighter. Her English was impeccable. Growing up she corrected me often, insisting on proper English. And even with an eighth grade education, she was sharp as a whip and in control and command at all times.

Aunt Rose was the only aunt who didn't machine gun me down with questions riddled with guilt. Where have you been? Why don't you visit more often? You're only staying for the afternoon? What about tomorrow? She was self-contained, never looking for more of my time than I could give. Aunt Rose never married. But she was the matriarch of the Cibella family, being mother to all of us.

She dished up the steaming escarole and beans, and we sat down to eat and talk.

"Tell me again about Grandma and Grandpa when they first came to this country."

"We were poor. Mama worked in a cigar factory making $3 a week. Ten hours a day, six days a week. Right in Newark, the factory was. They used to hand roll the cigars in those days and that's what she did. When I was born, she stopped working, but we always did 'home work.' Home work, you know, taking in sewing and beading.

"I remember when I was 5, she taught me how to make rosettes, those little crocheted flowers. We'd work together. She'd make the collars and I'd make the rosettes. Then Mama bought a second-hand sewing machine and taught me how to make doll clothes. My hands were just the right size to make those clothes."

I looked at her hands now and saw my own in a few years, thin and veined and spotted. I touched her hand. She let me linger for a few seconds and then slowly pulled away.

"Aunt Rose, how do you get your beans so creamy?" She looked at me with a rare but slight smile, her eyebrows raised halfway up her forehead, as though she were about to tell me a state secret.

"You mash up half the beans with a fork while they're cooking in the olive oil. That's the secret," and she gave me a satisfied nod. I made a mental note and mopped up the juices with some bread.

Now she really smiled. "I'll tell you something really bad that I did when I was a little girl."

"I was the one who had to pick up the 'home work' and deliver it when it was complete. One day I walked all the way to this place behind Haynes Department Store – all the way downtown, across the railroad bridge – they'd never let a child walk there today – to deliver the doll clothes we'd finished. I told the woman that my mother didn't want any work for that day because she wasn't feeling well. When I got home I told Mama there wasn't any work. I kept thinking of having a whole day to myself with no work to do. The next day after school when I got home the woman was sitting there in our apartment talking to Mama. She'd come to see her since I'd said she wasn't well. When she left I knew I was in for a spanking for lying. Mama asked me why I'd told that lie and I said I just wanted a day to do nothing. She started crying and apologized for working me so hard. I felt so bad that I never did that again. But she didn't spank me. She understood. She was wonderful, the best."

It was comforting to hear about my grandmother. I only remembered her as an old lady. She'd come to our house when I was young always carrying two bags full of food, vegetables from her garden and the occasional sweet. But she had a stroke when I was very young, and my only other memories are of her sitting in a dark flannel robe, her white hair like a halo around her very wrinkled face, her daughters trying to make her comfortable.

Rose Cibella, 16th birthday, 1920

Aunt Rose continued. "Everyone became attached to Mama. She helped everyone. She had great courage too. I remember a story being told around the apartment building. A little boy who lived in our building climbed up on the stove and lit some matches. He caught fire, and no one was courageous enough to grab him and put out the fire. But Mama did. She grabbed him and wrapped him in the apron she was wearing – you know those long, front aprons. Mama went to the hospital with that little boy still wrapped in her apron. The boy died anyway, but she tried to save him. Mama gave birth to twins just three weeks afterwards."

I dug into the roasted red peppers, piling them on a thick slice of crusty Italian bread, olive oil dripping onto my hand. I licked it off. The peppers were soft and sweet with little bits of burnt skin here and there. I ate with gusto. It made her happy to see me enjoy her food.

As the first-born she took on a lot of responsibility. She was helping to support the family at age 5, and that continued her whole life. She was also a second mother to her sisters. She knew she helped the family survive in this new country, and she was proud of it.

"Aunt Mary was born December 7, 1906, 25 months after me. Aunt Angie came next. She was a twin, you know, a little boy who only lived nine days. I remember he was wrapped up in a blanket and kept in the oven with the heat on and off to keep the right temperature. Aunt Angie was only five pounds, and he was less. Mama and Papa took him to the cemetery, just the two of them, carrying his little white casket on their laps. No one else went with them. Just the two of them."

Aunt Rose barely ate but she pushed the eggplant parmesan in front of me and went to cut some more bread. There's nothing in the world like a good eggplant parmesan with melted strings of mozzarella cheese dripping from your fork and the soft center of the eggplant surrounded by a crispy fried crust of bread crumb, egg and flour. Topped with tomato sauce and parmesan cheese it's the perfect combination of flavors and textures.

"People talk about how hard it is today being a working mother. Mama worked hard all the time. Another job she had was at the Houghton Chocolate Factory. She used to bring us home chocolates. But she worked hard and long. Six days a week, ten hours a day and she had to walk to work and back – a mile each way. I took care of all the kids. I remember combing everyone's hair in the morning getting them ready for school. I did it all. How they used to yell at their hair being pulled. I have to laugh when I think of it."

The sun came through the front windows and lit up the whole room. Aunt Rose and I moved to the overstuffed couch, and I admired her tatted doilies. She had a surprise for me and went into the bedroom to get six tatted coasters for my house in San Francisco. I fingered the tatted coasters, thinking of my grandparents. I knew I was reaping the rewards of all their struggles. I owed so much to them for making the long trip from Italy to Newark. I owed them a debt of gratitude, a debt that I realized too late to thank them properly. But Aunt Rose was still here, and I thanked her, not only for the coasters but for her hard work for the family. She brushed my words aside with the wave of her hand and got up to put the tea on.

She talked as she moved around the tiny kitchen.

"The summer when I was 13, Mama took me to apply for jobs. She didn't want me going alone. She took me to the Charms Factory and they hired me immediately because my hands were the right size. You had to hold seven charms and wrap them – all by hand in those days. I made $7 a week. That was good money, and I gave it all to my mother. When fall came and school started Mama decided I'd keep my job since it was such a help to the family. I was too young to quit school so she told them we were moving to New York. They believed her and I kept that job. I was so proud of myself. I remember when I gave my first paycheck to Mama. Uncle Rocco was there. He gave me 50 cents for being so good to my mother. I gladly left school and was happy I could help."

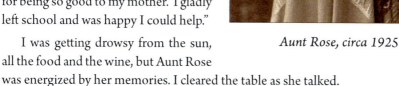

Aunt Rose, circa 1925

I was getting drowsy from the sun, all the food and the wine, but Aunt Rose was energized by her memories. I cleared the table as she talked.

"We were poor," she said again. "Papa worked for Public Service digging ditches for sewer pipes and water lines. He'd give his whole paycheck to Mama, and she'd give him an allowance. They had nothing when they came to this country. They came on borrowed money and, believe me, Papa paid it back a hundred times over."

I could hear the anger and resentment in her voice as she continued.

"The money and clothes he sent to Italy all those years. He didn't stop until I went to Italy and saw they were living better than we were. Mama would take clothes out of our closets and send them to Italy. They never saw Italy grow prosperous so they kept sending them things remembering how it was when they left."

Hearing Aunt Rose's anger, I asked if her Mama had a temper. I was thinking of my own mother and hoping to gain some insight into her anger which was forceful and unpredictable.

"Grandma had a lot of patience. It was Grandpa who had the temper. He would flare up easily. Mama had a way of calming him. With us she'd only threaten to get angry. She'd say things like: 'one of these days I'm going to get mad at you.' But when she was mad at us, she'd pinch us as we ran by her. But mainly I remember she was very patient."

She handed me a cup of tea and offered some Italian wedding cookies.

"I didn't make these myself," she confessed. "I told my neighbor you were coming and she sent these over."

We drank our tea. Her downturned mouth stayed in place, but her eyes told me how proud she was of me. I'd been the first to fulfill her dream for her family, college graduation and a master's degree. That was my gift to her, my part in the struggle: to accept the opportunities that her sacrifices allowed. We hugged at the door.

When I left, the hall, the elevator, the entrance, even the blocky concrete building looked different to me. This was Aunt Rose's home. She had given me the gift of connectedness to my history, to my family, to my memories. She had filled me with many of the comfort foods of my childhood, and she had given me the tatted coasters that I still held in my hand. I looked forward to her party the next day and seeing the rest of the family.

Aunt Rose's 90th Birthday

It must be overcoming so much adversity or it's the adventurous genes in all of us, but our family can throw a party! There are a lot of us, and Aunt Rose's gathering included 200 people, family and friends. My cousins and I, true to our wanna be movie-star selves that we perfected in the basement of 308 Clifton Avenue, were the entertainment. While everyone was having dessert, five of us slipped away to don nuns costumes and perform a song and dance to "Sisters." It was a tribute to all five Cibella "girls," all white-haired now, who sat together at the head table: Aunt Rose, 90; Aunt Mary, 88; Aunt Angie, 85; Aunt Cleo (my mom), 79; Aunt Eleanore, 74. Just as they'd done when we put on plays when we were young, they cheered and encouraged our antics. And we reveled in their attention.

At the end of the party, Aunt Rose called me over and handed me a small familiar looking box. I opened it and there was the ring I'd given her twenty years before as a thank you gift. Aunt Rose had loaned me money to go to college. I paid her back two years after I graduated and when I did, I gave her the ring she was giving back to me

Aunt Rose's 90th birthday, 1994, Cleo, Mary, Rose, Angie

now. I knew she was preparing for her death and tying up loose ends. Slipping the ring on my finger was the closing of a circle, the give and take and give back again of our family. I hugged her, feeling protective of her frail body. She died a year later.

For recipes in this section, see Chapter 10: Everyday Meals.

Mary Cibella Stefanelli (12/7/1906–11/8/1997)

Mary was the second of Tomaso and Camille's five daughters, born December 7, 1906. The opposite of Aunt Rose in every way, Aunt Mary was round and soft and seemingly unconcerned about anything. Her hair was often frizzy and out of control. She mostly sat at her kitchen table, dressed in a faded house coat or riotously colored mumu. She reminded me of the old Italian ladies who would sit at their windows all day watching the world go by. Aunt Mary sat in her kitchen watching for matches in her solitaire deck and looked up only to smile gently at all of us kids running through her house. She lived on the second floor of 308 Clifton Avenue with her husband, Victor Stefanelli, and her three daughters: Mary Ann, Camille and Johanna.

Victor Stefanelli served in the Navy during World War II. I think she fell in love with his uniform because she kept a picture of him in his white sailor hat and navy blues in her living room for as long as I remember. He had the typical sailor tattoo on his arm: a woman in a bathing suit positioned so she danced when he flexed his muscles.

"Show us your tattoo, Uncle Victor," we'd ask.

And he'd roll up his sleeve and make her dance for us.

When he left the Navy, he worked for Ballantine Brewery. The factory was in Newark. He told me he got to drink as much beer as he wanted. That was fine for a while until he stopped coming home after work and would stagger in at all hours. Aunt Mary always waited up for him with strong coffee and something to eat. When I read Homer's *Odyssey* in college about Penelope weaving every day and unraveling it at night, I thought of Aunt Mary. Patient and resigned. But she hadn't always been resigned. Early on in her marriage, she tried to leave Uncle Victor because of his drinking. She cried to her parents, wanting to return to their home.

"You made your bed, now lie in it," my mother told me Grandpa said to her.

They were harsh words and sent fear through me. The message to me was mistakes are not redeemable. You decide and are stuck with your decision for your whole life. It was a saying spoken often in our parochial immigrant community. The need for acceptance as well as the strictness of the Catholic Church gave added weight to immigrant propriety and sometimes came out in unsympathetic pronouncements.

Aunt Mary persevered just like Penelope. She and Uncle Victor remained married for almost 50 years. She was a good wife, a caring mother and a welcoming aunt. I loved Aunt Mary for her gentle ways as much as for her macaroni and cheese and morning pancakes.

Aunt Mary and Uncle Victor with Grandpa Cibella at their wedding, 1933

🍂🍂🍂🍂🍂

    In my mind Aunt Mary is associated with coffee. Her house always smelled of fresh brewed coffee. There was always a pot percolating on the stove. I'd wake up when I spent the night to the enticing smell of coffee and burnt butter. I knew Aunt Mary was up, drinking coffee, and busy making pancakes for me. We almost never had pancakes at my house and when we did, my mother would serve them with Karo syrup which she thought was healthier. But Aunt Mary practically drowned hers in delicious, sticky real maple syrup with butter floating in it. Her pancakes always had crispy edges. I'd take a bite, and the sponginess of the middle plus the crunchiness of the edges plus the dripping syrupy butter would turn the grayest New Jersey morning into sweet sunshine.

Aunt Mary also made great macaroni and cheese. There was no such thing as boxed mac and cheese like there is today. She'd make a large bowl of it, cooking the ditalini pasta separately and layering it with cheddar cheese, butter, bread crumbs and splashes of milk. In the oven it would crisp to a light brown on top.

She used a large Pyrex bowl that was yellow on the outside and white inside. It came from a set of nesting bowls that were all different colors, and this was the largest. I can still picture her cooking the macaroni and cheese. Her mumu that day was red with large orange flowers and green leaves on it. It flowed over her wide hips. She got out the macaroni pot and salted the water. While cooking ditalini well past al dente, she grated a big hunk of cheddar cheese. Sometimes she'd use Velveeta, which I loved, until I found out it was practically plastic. But Velveeta was so American, and I must admit, I wanted desperately to be American. Today she grated cheddar using the large holed side on the cheese grater.

I can see Aunt Mary shaking the ditalini in the colander.

"Get as much water out as possible," she directed.

Then she perched the shaken colander on the lip of the macaroni pan, buttered the bowl and began layering: macaroni, grated cheddar cheese, four or five dabs of butter, light dusting of Progresso Italian bread crumbs and a healthy splash of whole milk.

She didn't talk much. She just showed me, smiling as she repeated the layering three or four times. Finally came a top layer of cheese and a healthy sprinkling of bread crumbs. She put it in the oven at 350 degrees and set the timer for 40 minutes.

She poured herself a cup of coffee and sat down. I sat with her for as long as it was polite.

"Call me when it's done, Aunt Mary," I called over my shoulder as I headed downstairs to find my cousins.

And she did, dishing up a large bowl for me.

Angelina Cibella Aulise
(5/5/1909–12/11/2003)

Aunt Angie, 1989

Angelina, known as Angie, was the third Cibella child, born May 5, 1909. She was the twin whose brother died after nine days. One time, when I was 7 years old, she told me she still missed him.

"What do you mean?" I asked. "You were just a baby when he died."

"I've always felt someone was missing from my life," she told me.

"Oh," was all I said.

Aunt Angie was short and small and had the impish smile of a mischief-maker. I can remember her eyebrows shooting up, her eyes twinkling, her mouth forming an ironic twist of a smile as though she were seeing secret meanings to ordinary family situations. She liked to say the outrageous. I think it was her way of getting a reaction from her prim and proper sister, Rose, with whom she lived until she was 60. I enjoyed Aunt Angie's rebelliousness. She is the aunt who showed me what pushing the limits of immigrant propriety looked like. I see now the limits she pushed were quite harmless but, to me as a child, she was daring, bordering on reckless.

One Sunday during dinner, Aunt Angie announced she was going out on strike. Both she and Aunt Rose worked in the Tung-Sol factory in Newark. Aunt Angie was on the assembly line making light bulbs. Aunt Rose, a manager, disagreed entirely with the striking workers. She didn't say much, but her face said it all. Aunt Angie was not impressed by her disapproving look and began singing strike songs. I sat and listened to the arguing back and forth and, of course, to my Aunt Angie singing.

She didn't drink much, but when she did, she'd get a little tipsy, another behavior that seemed very bold to me and, therefore, I loved it. She married late in life to her next door neighbor, Edward Aulise. They were both in their 60s when they married. I never knew Edward very well. He nursed his first wife through cancer. Aunt Angie sympathized with him and helped him, and after his wife died, their relationship grew from friendship to romantic.

"The neighbors might think something was going on before she died," Aunt Angie worried to me.

*Grandpa Cibella, Aunt Eleanore, Aunt Mary, Aunt Rose,
and Aunt Angie, around 1960*

"Don't worry about it," a wise 27-year-old me advised her.

I called Aunt Angie three months before her 90th birthday. She said she was wobbly and needed a cane and sometimes a walker. She didn't get out much any more.

When I mentioned the time she went out on strike, she laughed in a self-deprecating way, and I could picture her waving it off as if to say, "it's nothing." But it was a highlight of her life, and she told me about it again.

"When the boss came to the factory window, we would burst into the song, *How Much is That Doggie in the Window?*" This memory really made her laugh.

"I'd walk into the factory with a hidden bell on me and purposely ring it as I passed Aunt Rose – to make her mad. Boy, did she get mad. Her face turned all red.

"Oh, I was bad in those days," she said.

She was on strike for two weeks, and they won a dime an hour. She said they never made up for that lost time. She couldn't remember what she was making before the strike in 1949. She did remember that she started out making 28 cents an hour in

1925. She asked me to hold the phone and came back with her check stub. Her pension from Tongsol was $1,029.12 a year. That's $85.76 a month.

"During the Depression, only one person in a family could work. By then there were three of us sisters working there. One was your mother. She had to leave, and I was forced to take five weeks off without pay. Aunt Rose, who was making the most, could keep her job. Married women were the first to be let go since it was presumed they had husbands to support them."

Unlike the rest of the Cibella sisters, Aunt Angie didn't cook. I know she loved polenta, so one time when I visited I made polenta with marinara sauce. I'd brought the coarse corn meal from California and reluctantly used store-bought canned tomatoes. I wished I could have brought some of my home-canned tomatoes but, being in glass jars, the airline nixed that. Her kitchen was small, ill-equipped. While Aunt Angie sat in the living room, I moved around her kitchen trying to familiarize myself with it. The dried basil and red pepper flakes looked old. I worried. I set the water to boil and measured out the polenta. I stirred in the polenta and listened to my aunts talk. What they said doesn't matter. The sound of their voices, even when they disagreed with each other vehemently, was familiar and comforting. I added salt and continued to stir.

When I served it, my fears came true. The herbs were old, the flavor a little flat. My aunts didn't seem to notice.

Grandma Cibella surrounded by three of her daughters and grandchildren

Eleanore Cibella Hockin (12/14/1920)

Eleanore, the fifth Cibella daughter, was the most "American" of my aunts. She married a non-Italian, quite unheard of at the time. Her husband, Kenneth Hockin, had blue eyes and fair skin. He was funny and outrageous. He had a bridge that held a tooth in place and would scandalize us children by pushing it out and making faces. The other men in the family were conservative, staid, proper, by comparison. But Uncle Kenny was outspoken, a bit of a rogue, a rascal, a prankster, large and athletic. We loved him! He was a Marine in the Second World War and had a picture of himself in uniform on a horse to prove it.

"How did you lose your hair, Uncle Kenny?" we'd ask.

"The Japanese army pulled it out. They grabbed my hair and dragged me around." We looked at him with wide eyes, believing every word, even when Aunt Eleanore would say "Oh, Ken" and roll her eyes.

He had hunting dogs and shot deer. He loved ice cream and would eat it by the gallon until he had a heart attack at age 55 and had to slow that kind of eating down.

Aunt Eleanore and Uncle Kenny had seven children: Roberta Hockin Lilley, Kennneth Hockin, Jr., Rosemary Hockin, Thomas Hockin, John Hockin, Christine Hockin Minopetros, and Gary Hockin. While Uncle Kenny was in the Marines, Aunt Eleanore, Roberta, and little Kenny lived in the attic apartment above us. Roberta would sneak down every morning at the crack of dawn, and we'd have a good old time until my father yelled for us to "keep it down." When we didn't, he'd get out of bed and come running.

Roberta would always hide in the closet. How did he know where she was every time?

"Rye Loaf," he'd demand, "get back upstairs."

She'd leave, her curly head of hair bouncing until the next morning when the whole routine would be repeated.

Roberta got into a lot of trouble, like the time she painted herself green and had to be washed down with turpentine, or the time she said she could fly and showed us, only to end up splitting her lip face down on the floor.

"Rye Loaf," my father would say, unable to suppress a smile, "What am I going to do with you?"

Aunt Eleanore was "American" in another way. She cooked hamburgers and mashed potatoes, "American food" unheard of in my mother's kitchen. Meat and potatoes, cold cuts, coleslaw, pickles, even hot dogs and buns slathered with mustard and sauerkraut. It was a different world of food, a far cry from the peppers and eggs, escarole and beans, macaroni of all sorts at my own house.

Aunt Eleanore loved polenta with sausage gravy. So when I visited her for her 90th birthday, I cooked it for her in her kitchen. At 90, she was still going to the gym three days a week, driving to visit friends and reading the paper every day cover to cover. She was an inspiration to me, and I wanted to know as much about her as possible. We sat down to eat, and I peppered her with questions.

"Oh, I don't remember much," she said but then, in true Eleanore style, proceeded to talk about her childhood, her parents, her children, grandchildren, and great grandchildren for a wonderful three hours.

"I don't remember a lot," she repeated, "really, except that we were rushed to Americanize. My children often ask why I can't speak Italian,

Aunt Eleanore and Roberta, 1943

and I tell them we were made to speak English and be proficient in it as soon as possible. Aunt Rose was the only one who had lessons in reading and writing proper Italian because she wrote letters to the family in Italy. She never wrote anything English or Italian without a dictionary by her side. That was Aunt Rose, doing everything properly. She taught me a lot. She'd say, 'stand with your shoulders back and don't shuffle your feet when you walk.' She taught me how to dress with style. She wanted me to look American, to not stand out as an immigrant. Oh, she was stylish, always with a scarf around her neck and a broach.

"She wouldn't let me read anything but good literature. I used to try and read those magazines about the Hollywood stars and gossip magazines, and she'd throw them away."

I stirred the polenta continuously to insure its creaminess while she washed the lettuce for our salad.

"I learned a lot from my sister, Cleo, too," she continued. "I was her first intern. She taught me everything about keeping house and being a good wife and mother. I owe her a lot."

She watched me stir and told me again that she couldn't get this perfectly ground corn meal anywhere around here. I promised her I'd continue sending it to her from California. Then she smiled and told me this story.

"One time I invited my future mother-in-law for dinner. Mama made polenta and Papa was furious. He said it was a shame to serve a guest peasant food. I wonder what he'd think now when it's served in all the best restaurants in New York City!"

The polenta was perfect, creamy with just the right amount of coarseness. Aunt Eleanore had made the sausage gravy beforehand. I dished up the polenta, covered it with tomato sauce and sausage, and set the streaming plates on the table. We sat down together. Between mouthfuls she continued.

"When Papa came to this country, I think it was 1903, he lived with his brother Angelo and his wife, Catherine. He lived there and so did Grandma when she arrived, five months later, until they had enough money to get their own place. Their first place was two rooms at 14 Garside Street."

"14 Garside Street. That's the first block of Garside Street," I said excitedly. "That was the heart of Little Italy," I told my aunt, as though she didn't know. I was excited because I'd read that Giordano's Bakery was at #13 Garside Street, the Italian language newspapers were printed at #4, Palagonia's Macaroni Store was at #12. This was a busy, crowded, neighborhood full of noisy children and people doing business and socializing at all hours of the day and night. And my grandparents were there in the thick of it, making their way in this country, raising their children, struggling to put food on the table and pay the rent. I was romanticizing all of this, I knew, but I couldn't help feeling a part of something bigger. Hearing about my grandparents expanded my world and gave me such pride!

"Yes, yes," she waved my research away.

"In 1929 Papa and Mama bought a house at 197 Garside Street. It was a three-family house, and he depended on the renters to help pay the mortgage. Because of the Depression, one of the tenants couldn't pay his rent. Papa fumed and yelled to Mama that he was going to go up and demand his money. When he came down, he was getting an extension cord. Mama asked what he was doing. He said, 'They have no electricity,' and he was sharing his electricity with them. Mama and Papa lost that house. People were having a hard time, and he couldn't put them out. After that they lived on Lake Street, but then Aunt Rose and Aunt Angie bought the house at 308 Clifton Avenue.

"Papa was very broad minded, liberal, and he had a good sense of humor. He was smart, too. He learned to play bridge, and we often played together. He also founded the St. Gerard Society."

I interrupted her to tell her I'd seen his name on a plaque honoring the men who founded the St. Gerard Society in St. Lucy's Church in Newark.

"He used to carry the statue during LaFest'. The statue made a special stop at our house when we were growing up. We'd pin money on the cloak," she said with pride.

She offered me some wine which had probably been opened a few months before and stored in her refrigerator ever since. I sipped to be polite. It wasn't vinegar but close to it.

"Mama had two brothers, and she lit up every time they came to visit. One was Uncle Rocco. The other was Fred, but his real name was Fortunado Lugano." Her eyes lit up. "Here's an interesting story. Fred was found as an infant on Mama's mother's doorstep in Caposele wearing fine clothes and laying in a basket. A dog kept barking outside, and that was how they found him before he froze to death. They named him Fortunate Dog, Fortunado Lugano."

Aunt Eleanore and Grandma Cibella, 1940

Afterwards, when I got back home, I looked up lugano. It's not in the Italian dictionary so maybe it's a dialect word or maybe it's just a made up story. But it's good in any case.

It was hard to interrupt Aunt Eleanore, but I managed, cleared her plate, and served a simple red leaf lettuce and balsamic vinegar salad.

"What about food when you were growing up? What did Grandma cook?"

"Mama was a great cook. I guess everyone thinks their mother is a good cook, but she really was. There was a pattern to her cooking:

"Sunday was the day Mama made gravy, a big pot of tomato sauce that would last the whole week. She made it with meat balls, sausage and braciole. Oh, she made the best braciole. She'd use a very thin cut of flank steak, sprinkle it with chopped garlic, basil, oregano, parmesan cheese and, of course, salt and pepper. I can still see her rolling the meat and wrapping it with string before putting it in the frying pan to brown.

"On Sunday there was always something special like bows and pot cheese or ravioli. Mama made ravioli from scratch. She had this big rolling pin that was more like a five-foot pole, and she rolled the dough out very thin. It was my job to press the fork around them to keep the ricotta in. She'd put a big clean sheet on a bed and lay the ravioli on it until it was time to cook them."

I interrupted my aunt, "I remember making ravioli with my mom when I was growing up." I remembered the anticipation of eating that light, delicate dough and plump dumplings of ricotta cheese all the while we were making them. The anticipation was almost as good as the eating.

"Monday was a thick soup like chicken or lentil soup or a jumble of vegetables like Jambought'. The jambought' she made right from her vegetable garden: zucchini, string beans, peppers, onion, potatoes and tomatoes all simmered with fresh basil and oregano. She'd send one of us to Giordano's for a big round loaf of Italian bread. We'd wipe up the juices with the bread."

My mouth watered just hearing about it.

"Tuesday was spaghetti, and the tomato sauce that was made on Sunday. We'd get our pasta from the macaroni store on Garside Street. They'd make it right there and dry it in the back room. The spaghetti wasn't like it is today, short and in boxes. When you bought it, it was long and wrapped in white paper. I'd carry it home trying to balance it on my head.

"Wednesday was some kind of greens day, like minest' and beans or string beans and potatoes or spinach and potatoes. We'd have that with a salad or broccoli rabe with garlic, olive oil and lemon slices.

"Thursday was 'fat macaroni' night. That meant ziti, rigatoni or mostacelli. With tomato sauce and meat, of course."

Friday: "We couldn't eat meat on Fridays back then. I don't remember any special recipe for fish because I never liked fish. But many of Mama's recipes were without meat, like polenta with marinara sauce or pasta fagioli or ceci and pasta or rice and peas or peas and pasta. Oh, those dishes were delicious. Considered peasant food, but so delicious.

"Saturday," she thought for a while, "I don't remember."

"I have a surprise for you," she said, smiling and rising from the table. She went to the refrigerator and brought out two large cannolis from an Italian bakery nearby. We dug into those creamy, sweet delights as she continued.

Aunt Eleanore is never lost for words so just as I thought the subject of food was exhausted, she became animated about lunches.

"Lunches were not like today – just grab something. Some of the best food was served at lunch. I came home for lunch even in high school. We had peppers and eggs, browned on both sides with thick slices of Giordano's bread. I had a friend whose mother used to make her lunch with white bread and even cut the crust off, but I had this great crusty Italian bread in thick slices. I can still picture Mama with the big round of bread under her arm slicing it. We had roasted peppers, potatoes and eggs, even broccoli rabe sandwiches dripping in olive oil."

*Grandma and Grandpa Cibella on their
50th wedding anniversay, 1954*

"If I could right now," I said to myself, "I'd run down to Giordano's and make a sandwich of roasted pepper and broccoli rabe," forgetting completely that I'd just had a filling meal.

"There was always a salad on the table. Grandma taught me to wash my hands carefully and then mix the salad with my hands – just oil and vinegar. And lots of fruit – always lots of fruit.

"We all ate around the table. It was pleasant, but we couldn't talk until after we finished our meal. Papa always said 'eating was communicating with death.' He chewed everything down to a fine powder. We kids used to tease him that he even chewed water. But after eating, we'd sit around and talk. Papa would have a glass of wine, and he and Aunt Rose would always argue about politics. But it was pleasant. It was obvious that Papa and Mama loved each other. They never fought, and once I heard her say 'stop that, Tomaso' because he was pinching her bottom.

"Did I tell you about our bootlegger?" she asked. Not waiting for an answer, she laughed and went on.

"At the 197 Garside Street house there was a wine press in the basement and Papa made his own wine. And we had our own private bootlegger! It was my godmother's husband, Jimmy Montana. I can still see the bottles lined up in the pantry. Mama would go to the pharmacy for flavorings to make anisette, for example. We didn't have a refrigerator until 1934, the year I graduated from St. Lucy's Grammar School. It was a Kelvinator run on gas, and Grandpa got a 25-percent discount because he worked for Public Service. Before that we had an ice box, and we had to put a card out whenever we wanted ice, and the ice man would deliver it. We had other delivery people: there was the bioncolino man who brought the bleach for washing clothes, the cooking oil man who brought the olive oil, the rag man, and the horse and wagon which brought around fresh vegetables and fruit for sale.

"Doing the laundry was hard. Mama would wash the clothes in tubs on top of the stove to boil the water. It was hard work stirring the clothes with a big wooden pole, and then she'd have to dress up in coat, hat and gloves to hang the laundry outside. She worked very hard. We got a telephone in 1937 because with Papa's job he needed to be available for emergencies. Of course, we had a party line and everyone in the building used it. I remember going out in the hall and calling to our neighbor, Jean, that the phone was for her."

"What do you know about your Papa and Mama's families in Caposele?"

"Oh, it's a sad story. Mama told me her mother, which would be my grandmother, was a widow and headstrong. She didn't want Mama to marry Papa. She thought he was beneath her. She told Mama that if she married Tomaso, she'd give her nothing and never see her again. She picked out another man for Mama to marry. One with a business and status. Mama refused to marry him."

Aunt Eleanore looked at me with a twinkle in her eye. "She told her mother that if she thought he was such a good match then she should marry him. When she married Papa, her mother kept her word. She gave her nothing – even her hope chest was taken away.

"Her mother also refused her an education because she felt women only needed to know how to do housework. Mama would steal her brother's books and try to teach herself to read.

"But when she was leaving Caposele to go to America, she told me that she got out of the wagon six times to hug and cry with her mother because she knew she'd never see her again. And it was true, her mother died a few short years after she came to the United States, and she never saw her mother again."

It was late when we finished talking. I tried to do the dishes, but she waved me away. At the door, I promised to send her more coarse ground corn meal. I went back to my mother's house, just five doors down, weighed down with the treasures of family history.

Five Cibella girls, 1994

Aunt Eleanore broke more of the traditional family values than her other sisters. Back then marrying "not your own kind" was considered dangerous and traitorous to the Italian-American community. Uncle Kenny was not only non-Italian, but he wasn't even a Catholic. It took a lot of courage for her to bring such a suitor home to meet her parents. But she did, and Uncle Kenny won their hearts as he did all of ours. He converted to Catholicism, which Aunt Eleanore insisted upon so their children could be baptized and receive their First Holy Communion and Confirmation.

They were the first in the family to move away from Newark and not to a close suburb like my mother, her sister, Cleo. They moved "down the shore" to Middletown to one of the new neighborhoods going up all over South Jersey. She cooked to "suit her husband" as she was taught to do by her mother. So her house looked, smelled and tasted more American.

Even so, family ties kept us all together. Most Sundays Aunt Eleanore and Uncle Kenny drove the hour each way so the whole family could be together. Predictably, Aunt Rose would cook a big meal; Grandpa would insist all us kids drink a small glass of wine mixed with water because it was "good for your blood." Aunt Angie would continue her brash, cheeky comments. We cousins rehearsed and performed our plays to our captive audience. It happened week after week, the family gatherings, always the same. It was a feeling of such comfort and certainty. Life seemed simple, secure and fun.

All the recipes mentioned in this section are in Part Two: Recipes.

The Castellano family, circa 1922

Chapter 2

The Castellano Family

Michael Angelo Castellano
(1885 to 11/25/1945)

Philomena "Fanny" Ilaria Castellano
(1887 to 8/11/1971)

Their children:

Nicolas Ilaria Castellano
(8/11/1908 to 9/11/1969)

Philomena "Mena" Volpe Castellano Fried
(10/26/1909 to 5/12/1990)

Michael Angelo Castellano, Jr.
(3/5/1911 to 1/16/1970)

Joseph John Castellano
(8/12/1912 to 1/31/1996)

Josephine "Dolly" Castellano Vuocolo
(11/17/1914 to 9/30/1997)

The Castellano side of the family, my father's side, was very different from the Cibellas, my mother's side. My father's father, Michael Angelo, who we called Grandpa Castellano, came to this country from San Fele, Italy, at age 2 with his parents. They traveled First Class. Because of that, they didn't go through the indignities of Ellis Island processing. I've heard the story that his father had been mayor of San Fele, but we can find no support for that. Michael Angelo was a lawyer, a City Attorney of Newark and a candidate for General Assembly of New Jersey in 1929.

My father's mother, Philomena Ilaria, who we called Grandma Castellano, was born in this country. She had a sixth grade education and could read and write. Michael and Fanny both transcended the immigrant mentality. Neither one was raised with the insults or uncertainty of poverty. Neither one suffered the embarrassment of illiteracy. With more disposable income, political connections and better education, the Castellanos were one step ahead of most Italians in Little Italy.

Grandma and Grandpa Castellano

Grandma and Grandpa Castellano were married in 1907 and had six children in quick succession: Nicholas (8/11/08–9/11/69), Philomena, known as Mena (10/26/09–5/12/90), Michael (3/5/11–1/16/70), Joseph (8/12/12–1/31/96), who was my father, and Josephine, known as Dolly, (11/17/14–9/30/97).

Michael Angelo Castellano (1885–1946)

On November 12, 1945, I received a letter from my Grandpa Castellano. I was 3 years old. It was written thirteen days before he died of stomach cancer. Although he died at home, he wrote it while at the Jersey Shore looking for a cure by "taking the waters."

Senator Hotel
Atlantic City, New Jersey
11/12/45

Mary Jo, Loretta, and Little Mena,
My dear Granddaughters and Sweethearts:

Grandpa Castellano is not feeling so good yet. The weather is bad, it is raining, and when it is raining at the seashore, sick people do not get better very soon, however, it will soon stop. It can't rain all the time, especially when Grandpa is waiting to get better so that I can be with you soon to buy you ice cream and take you out with my car.

Grandma Castellano is feeling good and she told me to tell you that she loves you all and she will soon be home to take you to her house where you can have lots of fun.

Do not worry I will be home next Saturday or Sunday of this week and will be feeling much better, and when I return I want to plant a nice kiss on your cheeks, so that I can show you all that I love you better and better every day.

Ask your Mama to help you, Mary Jo and you Loretta, to pray for me, so that I will get better, so that I can love you more and more dear sweethearts; of course, Little Mena cannot pray, but as soon as she can talk a little better she will be able to pray for me too. Please teach her to talk every day.

Be good to your Daddy and Mama and do not quarrel with each other, be good to Little Mena and Roberta, they are only babies and they both need your assistance.

Did you have a good time at the Mancini Birthday party last Saturday? I hope you did; when I took you, Mary Jo and Loretta, to the Mancini home you both looked beautiful.

Uncle Nick is with us and he sends you his love; he wants you all to be good girls and do not quarrel.

With love and affection,
Grandpa Castellano

"Let's go see the trolleys," he'd say before he got sick, knowing how much we loved watching those big, noisy engines clanging down the tracks on Bloomfield Avenue.

And there we were, my sister Mary Jo and me, all smiles, dressed exactly alike in starched, perfectly ironed dresses with matching bows in our hair.

"Just one more trolley, Grandpa," we'd beg. He complied happily before taking us to the ice cream parlor.

That's my Grandpa Castellano – kind, loving and patient.

My Dad told me a lot about his father as we drove people to the polls on cold November election nights. It would be dark out, and I'd stand in the back and look over his shoulder as he located the house of an elderly woman who needed a ride to her polling place. He'd laugh and tell me to "vote early and often" and chuckle. I laughed at that no matter how often I heard it. He'd pull up to a house and settle a neighbor into the front seat. While she was voting, he'd tell me things about my grandfather.

Grandpa Castellano campaign material, 1929

Grandpa Castellano came from a big family. He was the second of nine children. He was hit by a train during his childhood and lost the lower part of his left leg. My father used this as a lesson to me to stay away from railroad tracks. He told me that because of that, Grandpa Castellano wore a wooden leg from just below his knee. But he went through high school, college and law school.

While in New Jersey School of Law, in order to pay his tuition, he took a job in an Irish factory. Italians were not welcome so he applied under the Irish name, Costello. When the workers found out he was really Italian, they tried to run him out of the factory. He escaped by jumping out of a second story window into the Passaic River. My father, Joseph, his third son, used the same strategy when he applied for work at Standard Oil in 1937. That time it worked.

Italian men in the First Ward often congregated in social clubs with other men from the same region of Italy. They gathered to visit, play cards and drink. It was a place for men only, often smoke-filled store fronts with a few card tables for pinochle. They'd hold meetings once a week and pay dues for the upkeep of the club. They planned church, family and political activities.

These clubs were a big part of the Newark political machine of the Democratic Party. It's where candidates were chosen to run for local election and organize "get out the vote" and other election activities.

Grandpa Castellano belonged to the Caposelesi Club. He was a gregarious man who was often out late with his cronies, smoking big fat cigars and ordering beer by the pail. He was well respected as a City Attorney, and it was in this gathering of men that he was chosen to run for General Assembly of the state of New Jersey. He wasn't elected, but he made the whole family proud, and he made "Castellano" a household name, at least in Newark.

It was from Aunt Mena that I learned what a blow his death was to the family. Every sadness, disappointment or slight she felt, according to her, wouldn't have happened if her father was still alive. He was her protector. He was the one who softened his wife's strict ways for all the children. He was the center of the family and when he died, the center was lost. Uncle Mike and Aunt Dolly lost their footing, leaving the family to go to Florida for a while. They never recovered the sense of stability that their father provided. Uncle Nick, the oldest child, was looked upon as the head of the family, but he was distracted by establishing his career, nursing his sick wife and raising his child when she died. It was their fourth child, Joseph, my dad, who took on the everyday decisions of this large extended family. He never felt fully prepared for the responsibility, but he accepted it. After Grandpa's death, Grandma and all his siblings looked to him to provide the centerpiece that once had been held by his father.

Philomena 'Fanny' Ilaria Castellano (1887–1971)

Philomena Ilaria Castellano, known as Fanny, was born in the United States to Italian immigrant parents. Her mother died when she was a baby, and her father went back to Italy, leaving her to be raised by her mother's cousins. When her father came back to this country, he had a new wife and another daughter named Minnie Ilaria. For some reason he never integrated Philomena into his new family. I think of that now when I remember the tinge of sadness in her eyes even when she smiled. I don't know much about Fanny's life before she became a grandmother, but her life as a grandmother is the role model I turn to again and again when I am with my grandchildren today.

Grandma Castellano holding Uncle Nick, 1908

Fanny was a large woman. She wore long, pink, boned corsets to hold in her great weight. I was often called upon to help her fasten the rows of hooks and eyes or pull the laces tightly to her body. She would huff and puff while getting all of this on. And she did it every day.

"Dr. Filipone told me I have to lose weight," she'd lament each time she saw her doctor. "Your Grandma is fat," she'd tell us.

"No, you're not, Grandma," we'd cry, alarmed that we'd see her melt away. "And besides, grandmas are supposed to be fat." She liked hearing that, and before long she'd say her familiar, "I think I'll have a little nibble." And she'd go to the kitchen for a thick slice of Italian bread and butter.

As an adult, even in the 1960s, my sister Mary Jo would take her to be fitted for new corsets. When most young women were burning their bras, she was true to her Victorian image of a woman and had new corsets made each year.

Grandma Castellano was always stylishly and properly dressed. She chose her clothes carefully every day, including stockings and lace-up high heeled shoes. She never went out without a hat and gloves. Grandma believed that people treat you according to how you look. She lived up to her social status as the wife of an attorney even long after Grandpa died. She had beautiful taste, and it gave her a sense of confidence. She showed the world how she wanted to be treated by her demeanor and the clothes she wore. Her face was powdered, her nails were buffed. She always carried a linen handkerchief.

Grandma ruled the roost and commanded her children with great authority even when they were fully grown, married with children of their own.

"Joe, go to the store for me," she'd demand as soon as we entered her house.

"What do you need, Ma?" my father replied like an 8-year-old boy.

Aunt Dolly called her an "old battle-ax," behind her back, of course.

But to her grandchildren, she was loving and dedicated. When Mom and Dad let us sleep over at Grandma's

Grandma Castellano with Aunt Dolly in the background, circa 1934

house, we not only had Grandma, but Aunt Mena and Aunt Dolly all to ourselves. We had the run of the house, and we could do no wrong.

"Oh, my, how beautiful you are," Aunt Mena would exclaim, her thin eyebrows arched, a wide smile on her lipsticked mouth. Her closet was at our disposal. Aunt Dolly's too. Their closets were full of colorful circle skirts, belted dresses of silk, organza, wool and taffeta, silk blouses, straight skirts with kick pleats in the back. Their drawers were loaded with rhinestones, pearls, gold and silver chains, bright beads and colored stone jewelry. We wore padded strapless bras, off-the-shoulder blouses, skirts that dragged on the floor and necklaces by the dozens around our necks. We wore high heel shoes, hats with veils, brooches, scarves, and always a pocketbook on our wrist. We used tons of their bubble bath, oils, powders, perfumes. And the make-up: foundation, rouge, bright blue eye shadow, lipsticks in what seemed like hundreds of shades. We pranced like models through the house. Grandma would chuckle. She sat and watched our parade of outfits as proud of us as though we were on a New York runway.

She thought the world of us. She used to love watching the Miss America contest on TV. She'd watch the finalists pass by on the screen and say incredulously after each one: "My granddaughters are prettier than that."

On those overnights she'd make our favorite dishes: Rice balls (arancini) stuffed with mozzarella, or peas and pasta, or stuffed artichokes.

One of my favorite memories of Grandma is going to the cemetery with her each week. We'd pile into Dad's car and drive there, picking up flowers from a vendor outside the gates. I can still see Grandma bending over to pick up leaves and small twigs from Grandpa's grave.

Grandma Castellano with Lorrie and Mary Jo, 1943

"Joe, those flowers need to be moved a little," she'd order my father.

We kids would wander off among the graves. It was a quiet park, almost empty of people, our own private playground. In the fall, the leaves would be bright red and yellow. In winter the trees would be skeletons. In spring and summer there were dogwood trees, beautiful white blossoms tinged in pink. Soon we were running, climbing over the replica of the Pieta and putting flowers into the outstretched hands of the Sacred Heart or Michael the Archangel. Afterwards, we'd go to Applegate's in Upper Montclair for mint chip ice cream.

"Your Grandpa would love to be here with you," Grandma would say.

Grandpa and Grandma Castellano at their dinner table with some of the family, 1940

    Grandma's dining room was full of heavily carved dark wood furniture. The table sat twelve comfortably. A pad was put down to protect the table top, and over it was placed one of Grandma's white table cloths, always starched and perfectly ironed. Her china, from Bavaria, had a three-inch-wide rim of 22-karat gold around each plate with a painted bunch of flowers in the middle, and each place was set with crystal goblets and silver-plated cutlery. Everything sparkled.

    When all the family sat down to dinner, large hand-painted Italian pottery platters filled with food lined the middle of the table. Grandma was at the head presiding over the meal that she'd spend hours preparing, and in her hand was the serving spoon.

    Grandma's serving spoon is the one I still use today. It's shaped like a shell and is the perfect size and shape for dishing out bows and pot cheese, my favorite dish. Bows with pot cheese is pure comfort food, creamy, rich, seasoned ricotta cheese mixed into the tomato sauce and steaming farfalle pasta. She'd dish it up with her spoon, and every time I see that spoon I remember Grandma and her bows and pot cheese.

    I have three items from my grandmother: her serving spoon, one of her gold-rimmed dinner plates, and her wedding band. I wear Grandma Castellano's white gold ring along with my own wedding band. The engraving is too worn to read.

    "Oh, it can be fixed," she said when the glass-topped coffee table broke into tiny pieces because I banged a toy too hard.

    "You didn't mean it" and "What can Grandma get you, sweetheart?" she asked when I cried.

Philomena "Fanny" Ilaria Castellano was born in 1887 and died at age 83 in 1971.

When she died, in her refrigerator was a large bowl of meatballs that had been simmered in tomato sauce. We came home from her funeral, cooked up some macaroni, and ate her parting gift to us.

The recipes mentioned in this section can be found in Chapter 10: Everyday Meals.

Nicholas Ilaria Castellano (8/11/1908–9/11/1969)

Uncle Nick and Aunt Julia, 1941

When I was very little, Uncle Nick would come visit us after work at least once a week. He'd walk from the bus stop, hat on, briefcase in his hand. When I'd see him, I'd run, and he'd open his arms to catch me.

One day I ran to show him my new red shoes and how fast I ran in them.

"Red shoes run faster," he said sagely.

Nicholas Castellano, the first of Michael and Philomena's five children, was born August 11, 1909. He was tall and handsome. He wore a thin mustache, fine wool three-piece suits and a fedora. He married Julia Ferrari, a beautiful, flamboyant blonde from a New York banking family. For her wedding, she wore an ice blue satin gown. She was a fur coat, platform shoe wearing, glamorous woman. She wore beaded dresses and rings with large stones. I idolized her. My mother got me to drink eggnogs as a child by telling me I'd grow up to have blonde hair like Aunt Julia. It worked every time.

Aunt Julia (on the right) with Mary Jo on her second birthday, 1942

Nick followed his father into law and eventually became Chief Magistrate of the Superior Court in Newark, New Jersey. He had a group of cigar smoking, big drinking men friends. They rallied around him to push his political career, and eventually he ran for mayor of Newark. He didn't win, but like his father, his was a household name.

My brother, Joe, remembers visiting Newark in 1964 when he was 8 years old during the time Uncle Nick was running for mayor. Joe was at Grandpa Cibella's when a car with a large bull horn came down the street blaring "Vote for Hugh Addonizio for Mayor." Addonizio was Uncle Nick's chief rival. With the enthusiasm of a young boy, Joe yelled, "Don't vote for that bum!"

Mom, Dad and Aunt Dolly quickly quieted him down.

"Never yell things like that." Dad's tone was urgent.

"You never know who's listening," Aunt Dolly added. Newark politics must have been rough in those days.

Aunt Dolly told me how much fun she had sitting with supporters on the back of a convertible singing campaign songs for her brother to the tune of "Downtown," by Petula Clark. My brother, Joe, only remembers one line of the song:

"Judge Castellano is the man to elect to go to City Hall – Downtown."

When Aunt Julia became pregnant with their first child, her sister-in-law, Cleo, who was my Mom, took her to all her prenatal doctor's appointments. During one visit in the ninth month of pregnancy, the doctor handed my mother an X-ray. On it was stamped: DEAD FETUS.

"I looked at the X-ray. I looked at the doctor. I looked again at the X-ray. Julia looked at it and continued to smile. She hadn't noticed the horrifying words stamped on it. The doctor said nothing; I didn't know what to do. Did I read it right? Why wasn't he saying anything?" When my mother told me this story years later, she was still confused by it.

The baby was a still birth. A great tragedy for Nick and Julia. A year later their daughter, Angela, was born healthy.

One night when the Castellanos were gathered at our house for a birthday celebration, the women were urgently whispering and kept disappearing into the bathroom with Aunt Julia. Later my mom told me Aunt Julia had a lump on her breast that she wanted to show the women in the family. She'd been too scared to go to the doctor. My mother insisted and took her the next day. Within days, she had a mastectomy.

Uncle Nick named Chief Magistrate in Newark, New Jersey, 1952

"We have to pray for Aunt Julia," Mom told us. "Make a novena, please."

"Is she okay? She looks fine to me," I'd said.

"We won't know for five years."

When the disease advanced in spite of radiation treatments, Angela started staying at our house every weekend. She was like another child to my parents and another sister to us.

I watched Aunt Julia waste away, and her dark roots overcome her glorious blonde hair – my beautiful, full-of-life, stylish aunt of the platform shoes and fur coats, the veiled hats and flowers in her hair. One day, while sitting with her as she was dying, she asked me to pick out a bottle of perfume from her dresser. I picked a flowery, sweet-smelling, pale yellow one. "That's for you," she said.

When Aunt Julia died, Uncle Nick became quiet, almost mute with grief. Grandma Castellano moved into his house to raise Angela. Later Aunt Dolly did the same to help.

Like his father, Uncle Nick spent a lot of time with his friends at the Caposelesi Club. His mother and siblings criticized this choice. They thought he should spend more time with the family. When I would choose to go out with friends rather than family, my mother would call after me in a derogatory tone as I walked out the door,

"Zio Nicol!" (Uncle Nick in Italian.) I didn't know whether to feel pride or shame.

Philomena "Mena" Volpe Castellano Fried
(10/26/1909–5/12/1990)

Philomena Castellano Fried was born in 1909, the second child born to Michael Angelo and Philomena. She was the aunt of Yankee Stadium, Rockefeller Plaza, the Rockettes, and Flaming Alaska.

"It's Lady's Day at Yankee Stadium, let's go!" She was a big fan and inspired loyalty to the Yankees in me to this day.

And we'd take a bus to Newark Penn Station. Then a train to New York Penn Station. Get off at 34th Street and Herald Square. Then take the subway to 161st Street and River Avenue in the South Bronx. Yankee Stadium. The tickets were half price to ladies, so we dressed up and took our seats to watch such greats as Joe DiMaggio, Mickey Mantle, Phil Rizzuto, Yogi Berra, and Whitey Ford. We ate hot dogs, ice cream and cotton candy, waved our pennants and cheered for our team. On the way there, we sang

Take me out to the ball game…

The Yankees never lost to my memory. They were the kings of baseball, and I was glad they were our team. In 1952 when the Yanks played the New York Dodgers, we saw Roy Campanella, Pee Wee Reese, and Jackie Robinson.

Afterwards we'd go to Horn and Hardart's Automat, a glass and chrome wonder. Rows of small see-through dispensers lined the walls. Coin in, turn knob, glass door springs up, pull out your choice. And what a choice: sandwiches, macaroni and cheese, baked beans, beef stroganoff, mashed potatoes and, best of all, slices of pies of all kinds, ice cream, rice pudding and cookies. It was a hungry kid's dream palace.

Sometimes we'd go to Radio City Music Hall to see the Rockettes. They'd put on a lavish stage production just before the movie. Fifty girls synchronizing kick after kick in short skirts, top hats and fish net stockings. I wanted to be on that stage with all those bright footlights and glitter. Those dancers and the romantic movies that followed filled my dreams and still do to this day. Taking tap dancing lessons as a kid was the closest I've gotten except for the "flash mob" I organized for my 70th birthday celebration, the Rockettes still influencing me.

The Rockettes were a Christmas treat, and afterwards we'd go to Rockefeller Plaza to have lunch in a restaurant with large glass windows so we could watch the ice skaters gliding around the huge Christmas tree. At the end of the meal, the waiter would approach the table with a Flaming Alaska. It was an amazing sight, Aunt Mena smiling broadly at being able to present to her nieces this wonder of wonders, ice cream on fire. Aunt Mena had an imagination bigger than her world of Newark, New Jersey. She did her best to introduce it to us.

Aunt Mena married late in life. The reason was not that she couldn't find a boyfriend. It was that Grandma criticized her every choice. No one was good enough. For many years she tried to please her mother and broke off with men she liked because of what her mother said. Years later, when she met Bert Fried, she kept the relationship a secret until she was engaged and until she felt that nothing her mother said could dissuade her.

Aunt Mena, age 21, 1930

Uncle Bert was many years her junior, and she knew this would cause a lot of gossip and raised eyebrows. The rules and expectations about who is acceptable to marry, so common in our family, were particularly suffocating to Aunt Mena. It took her until she was 65 years old to finally stand up for her own happiness.

When Uncle Bert died, she decided to move to California. She was 74 years old. Although she lived there just a few years before returning to New Jersey, it took courage and imagination, some said folly, to pick up and move across country. But by that time, and with her mother dead, she found the world opening up to her and the bravery to follow her dreams.

Perhaps she was right. If her father had lived, her life would have been very different.

Michael Angelo Castellano, Jr. (3/5/1911–1/16/70)

Michael Castellano is the third of Michael and Philomena's children born March 5, 1911. Uncle Mike is my hyphenated uncle: devil-may-care, non-conformist, mischief-maker, easy-going, free-and-easy, slap-bang-adventurer. He was the wanderer, the vagabond, the unorthodox rascal. He exasperated the other adults in the family, but we kids loved him. He was fun and unpredictable. When he joined a family gathering, always late, the party started.

Uncle Mike, right, with Grandpa and Grandma Cibella at Mom and Dad's wedding, 1939

One Christmas Eve with the house full of the Castellano clan, twelve of us were waiting for Uncle Mike so dinner could begin.

"Where's Mike?" Grandma Castellano complained impatiently. "We should start without him!" and "That boy will be the death of me."

The house smelled of the traditional seven fish dishes of Christmas Eve. Mom was tossing the baccala and Aunt Julia arranging her shrimp scampi on a large square platter. Candles burned, Christmas tree lights flickered. Santa was coming later that evening to hand out gifts. The dining room table was set with Mom's best china and silver. A gallon of homemade red wine that Mr. Dellano, our landlord, gave to my father in exchange for doing his taxes, sat on the kitchen counter. The adults were sipping and complaining about Uncle Mike, wondering if he was going to show up at all.

We heard his footsteps coming up the stairs, and we kids ran to meet him. He usually had a big hug for us, but this night his arms were full. He carried a large butcher paper-wrapped package in both his arms. It was bulky and heavy looking. Uncle Mike was a thin, wiry person. He and my father, his brother, looked a lot alike: dark wavy hair and deep dimples on both cheeks when they smiled. But my dad was serious, responsible, the one my grandmother could depend on. Tonight Uncle Mike staggered into the kitchen under his heavy load, demanded that the kitchen table be cleared and gently laid his bulky package down.

"Where have you been?" Grandma scolded, smiling, happy to see him.

"Oh, Mom," he waved her off, giving her a kiss on the cheek.

We gathered around. Mom turned on the cappellini water to boil, finally able to get dinner on the table. But it wasn't to be that easy.

Uncle Mike unwrapped his package and there laying on our kitchen table was a complete, very large pig. I say complete because the eyes were still in the head and open.

My mother slapped her forehead, "Oh Madonna mia," and turned off the boiling water. My father just shook his head.

"Mike, are you crazy? What are we supposed to do with it?" Grandma asked in that gravelly voice she had when she was undone, her sense of knowing totally destroyed.

"Put an apple in its mouth," was my suggestion. Everyone just looked at me.

Uncle Mike started dancing around the table, twirling his sisters Mena and Dolly and trying to get Grandma to smile. She was having none of it, but we kids joined in dancing around the pig in the middle of the table. Mike was pretty tipsy and his dance morphed into a strip tease starting with his shoes. He took one off singing ... *A Pretty Girl is Like a Melody* ...

Off came the other. Mom laughed. Aunt Dolly clapped. We kids danced with him. His socks came off next. First one and then the other. He laughed so hard, he couldn't stand up.

We eventually sat down to our traditional Christmas Eve dinner, and Santa came, and the presents were given out and opened. I don't remember what happened to the pig. I know we didn't eat it. It was Christmas Eve, a no meat day.

🐖🐖🐖🐖🐖

For a short time after his father died, Uncle Mike moved to Florida where he met and married the love of his life, Norma Carr. He hid his marriage from the whole family. Each February, we visited him in Florida to get away from New Jersey's icy weather. Even then, he hid Aunt Norma and Linda, her child from a previous marriage. Mom and Dad would talk quietly on the long ride home speculating about the woman's clothes in the closet and toys scattered around the outside of their trailer. As indifferent as he seemed to the family code of conduct, he was still afraid of his family's disapproval.

"All this while he's been married and I didn't even know. What am I going to do with that boy?" Grandma asked an invisible jury when he finally called to tell her.

All of us kids were very excited when we learned Uncle Mike decided to move with his family back to New Jersey. He said he'd arrive at our house at dinner time. We waited. And we finally ate. And we waited some more. Disappointed, we went to bed. In the middle of the night the phone rang.

"Joe, can you send me some money," he sheepishly asked my father. "I got pulled over in Georgia. My car isn't registered."

His carefree attitude got him in a lot of trouble. His drinking didn't help. He had a hard time keeping a job. Our close-knit family jumped in to rescue him time after time. Uncle Nick bought a tavern which Uncle Mike ran. My Dad did the books whenever Uncle Mike could supply him with numbers. Many nights Grandma sent his dinner over.

Uncle Mike and Aunt Norma had eight children: Linda, Theresa, Michael, Eddie, Betty, Tony, Nicky and Shawna. The whole family helped raise them. Aunt Norma suffered from a recurrent major depression, the kind that sucks the energy out of a person. Theresa, their second child, stepped in and became "mother" as her mother's mental illness progressed and her father worked long hours at the tavern.

Aunt Norma, 1950

The last time my dad and Uncle Mike were together in 1969, Uncle Mike pulled my dad aside, "If something happens to me, would you take Michael and Eddie to live with you?" My Dad reassured him he would. He must have had a premonition because a year later, he died suddenly. Uncle Mike loved his children more than anyone and tried to make plans as best he could. When he died, the family jumped in. Linda married. Theresa went to live in Uncle Nick's house with Grandma. Michael and Eddie came to our house in Texas, and the four youngest went to live with Aunt Norma's sister in California. It was sad for my cousins, who were close-knit, to be separated. And sad for the whole family.

Uncle Mike made us all laugh. All the children in the family adored him. He was one of us and never grew up completely. The adults loved him even while shaking their heads in wonder at his shenanigans. We didn't rely on him, but he was the one everyone hoped would show up at family gatherings.

Recipes mentioned in this section are in Chapter 11: Christmas Eve.

Josephine "Dolly" Castellano Vuocolo
(11/17/1914–9/30/97)

The Castellano Girls Go To Ellis Island

Aunt Dolly turned 80 in 1995. I asked her how she wanted to celebrate.

"Don't make a big deal out of it," she said uncharacteristically because Aunt Dolly loved a party.

"I love the commotion when we're all together," she'd say, her curly black hair totally out of control.

Years before: "Let's go down the Shore" and off we'd go speeding down the Garden State Parkway. She used the New Jersey State Police as her personal assistants. If she needed directions, she waved them over. When stopped for some infraction, she'd flirt and casually drop her brother's name. It always worked.

"Are you really the Judge's sister?" they'd ask, smiling and flirting back.

She loved to party with her nieces and nephews. We treated her like a contemporary, and she played the adult supervisor with a mixture of pretend admonition and knavish smile.

"You kids are crazy," she'd say when we'd ask her who she was in love with this week.

"No party?" I said into the phone.

"No party. Who wants to celebrate getting old? I want a small, quiet birthday."

"We've got to do something!" I insisted.

"Oh, okay," she said as though the pressure was too much. She just wanted to be coaxed.

We decided to take the ferry to Ellis Island to see the names of our family engraved on the Immigrant Wall of Honor.

We arrived at the dock in Lower Manhattan. It was a clear, sunny November day. A crisp breeze brought the smell of the ocean. The seagulls squawked overhead. The pigeons ate bits of popcorn at our feet.

"What! Did you tell the whole world?" Aunt Dolly rolled her eyes, trying hard to hide her excitement and pleasure when Lucia, Katie, Terri, Mike, Evelyn, Pam, Pat, Angela, and two of Terri's grandchildren showed up on the dock.

Aunt Dolly, holding Angela at her christening, 1948

Lucia, my second cousin, is a true Castellano. I told her about our plan. Just like Aunt Dolly, she cannot stay away from a party. She'd spread the word to her cousins, second cousins, second cousins once removed and grandchildren. Lucia whispered to me that Toni and her daughter, Julia, were supposed to bring a cake. They were nowhere in sight so we boarded the ferry without them.

The ferry was packed, the children ran around, the parents called after them. Aunt Dolly said, "Oh, I love the commotion."

It was cooler on the island, a breeze made us pull our coats closer. We followed the American Immigrant Wall of Honor, a long, curved monument engraved with over 700,000 names honoring the first immigrants from a family. We found the name of Tomaso Cibella with no problem. We looked for the name of her father, my paternal grandfather, and found three Michael Castellanos.

"Oh, my feet hurt. I need coffee." This was too tame for our 80-year-old aunt.

We abandoned the search for Michael Angelo Castellano and went looking for the cafeteria. The path led us through the Immigrant Museum, full of life-size photos of long lines of men, women and children carrying bundles, looking worried. I silently thanked my grandparents for all they'd given me. Tears welled up in my eyes as we walked through the same rooms they had many years before.

✥✥✥✥✥

E-mails 17 years later:

Lorrie to Lucia: Lucia, what do you remember about Ellis Island and Aunt Dolly's birthday?

Lucia to Lorrie, cc Toni: We ordered the cake from a well known Italian Bakery in New York City. We did not realize when ordering it how big it was. Kate picked it up, and we took it on the ferry with us. We met Toni and Julie at the ferry dock and all went together. We had to explain to people what we were doing as we bumped into them trying to see around the cake. The cake was so big it needed its own seat. We also had champagne and plastic flutes. Toni, do you remember more?

Toni to Lucia and Lorrie: The cake was from Veniero's at 11th Street and First Avenue. It is their famous cannoli cake. It has a ricotta filling (as everyone knows) instead of the usual whipped cream or butter cream.

Lucia, your memory is not accurate, I'm sorry to say. I remember the story of the cannoli cake on the ferry, but we were not with you. We got there very late because my daughter's jeans HAD to be washed and dried before we left. That is why we couldn't find anyone at first when we got there so we headed for the cafeteria.

Lucia to Toni and Lorrie: I just realized that with Toni not being with us on the ferry, Kate and I can make up any story we like. Not only that but Tim (Lucia's husband) who has by far the most vivid account of the "Castellano Girls Go To Ellis Island" is also free to enter the fray, though he was not a party to the event.

Tim to Lorrie: Okay, I wasn't there, so my memories are unsullied by bumptious facts. The cake was massive. Dolly, who had not wanted a fuss, blushed again and again and again as each wave of newcomers arrived in the cafeteria, were given cake by Toni and Julie, and sang Happy Birthday. Multiple efforts to muster pilgrims for a final assault on the Wall of Names failed for lack of a quorum until finally the call for the last ferries to Manhattan and the mainland put an end to the party. It was glorious. It was epic. It was legendary. The memories are indelible. I wish I'd been there.

✥✥✥✥✥

The cafeteria on Ellis Island is a large room surrounded by windows from floor to ceiling. It seats a couple of hundred people easily. It was full. Among those 200 or so people were Toni and Julie, saving us a table. The cake sat in the middle of it. It truly was enormous. We toasted Aunt Dolly with champagne in plastic flutes and started singing *Happy Birthday*. Within seconds, the whole cafeteria joined in. I looked around at all those smiling people willing to join the party. People sang and whistled and came up to wish Aunt Dolly a happy 80th.

"You kids are crazy," she said waving a hand in front of her face, smiling and pretending she didn't like all the attention.

We served cake to everyone there and still had some left for the next seating.

On the ferry ride back we sang the old '40s songs:

*Gee, ain't it great after being out late,
walking my baby back home…*

and

*Fly me to the moon
And let me play among the stars…*

our arms around each other's waists swaying with the roll of the boat. We passed the Statue of Liberty. Salty spray splashed the windows. Seagulls glided. It was Aunt Dolly's 80th. She sat back happily.

"You kids," she said shaking her head. "This is your idea of a small, quiet celebration?"

Aunt Dolly partying in California, 1992

🐞🐞🐞🐞🐞

Aunt Dolly was always the "baby" of the family. She never grew up, really. Because of this she drove her sister, Mena, crazy. She seemed to get away with a lot, and Mena was always resentful that she didn't pull her own weight. But Aunt Dolly didn't feel like she had to. She was so cute with tightly curled black hair, a small slender figure and an easy laugh. She had a million friends. She was a big flirt with the men.

Aunt Dolly married twice. The first time she eloped to Red Bank, New Jersey, with a handsome blond sailor named Lonnie Lee. It was an impulsive thing to do, and she regretted it almost immediately. It was annulled. Her second marriage was to Joe Vuocolo. She never divorced him, but the marriage lasted only two or three years. It was stormy and ended in a dramatic fight.

Her clothes were spectacular. Long full skirts, some sequined, some embroidered, colorful silk blouses, cinch waist belts that showed off her lovely figure. Cashmere sweaters, beaded sweaters, shrugs, a curly lamb's wool coat in silver, platform heels in purples, prints and straw. She wore large pieces of silver jewelry and flowers in her hair.

"Can I have your gold lamé bathing suit when you die?" I'd ask her in all seriousness.

She'd laugh, knowing she'd never die.

She and my mother had a contentious relationship. I think she was jealous of my mom who seemed to have everything Aunt Dolly wanted but didn't know how to get: a home of her own, a reliable husband, many children. More than that, Mom had the perseverance that Aunt Dolly seemed to lack and that's so necessary to fulfill dreams.

She competed with my mother for our love. She often won, too, just because she was loving, nonjudgmental and generous with us. Her love for her nieces and nephews was the only constant in her life.

I always felt Aunt Dolly had a secret, but no matter how many times I asked her or how I phrased it, she never relinquished it. At her funeral in 1997, I spoke to her many friends who were there, moving quietly from one to another and questioning them in whispers.

"You didn't hear this from me," was the repetitive refrain.

And out came the story:

Always the one who wanted to be cajoled and pleaded with, she carried this over into her love life. She was used to being the center of attention and catered to. When the man she loved proposed to her, she coyly refused, thinking he'd run after her as so many other men had. She'd have the pleasure of the chase. And the power of keeping him guessing. But they were cut from the same cloth, it seems. He didn't chase her. He was angry. When she tried to make up, he refused her advances and left for military service in Italy. There, out of spite, he married an Italian girl and brought her home.

He was married and stayed married. But that didn't end it. They carried on a secret love affair well into old age. She loved him with a passion heightened by the presence of secrecy. And she got what she wanted, the constant chase. Their trysts took away her ability to commit to anything or anyone else.

When I heard this story from one friend after another at her funeral, the suspicion I had became a reality. I felt saddened for her by the weight of this secret. I wish she had confided in me so that the loneliness I imagine she felt could be shared. I could have given back to her what she had always given to me: nonjudgmental love.

Mom and Dad's wedding, May 30, 1939

Chapter 3

The Uniting of Both Families: Our Parents

Loretta "Cleo" Cibella Castellano
(4/19/1915 to 1/18/2011)

Married on May 30, 1939

Joseph John Castellano
(8/12/1912 to 1/31/1996)

Mom: Loretta 'Cleo' Cibella Castellano
(4/19/1915 – 1/18/2011)

Like creating a satisfying relationship with my mom, making pizza with her was a difficult and frustrating undertaking. But once I succeeded, the feeling was exhilarating.

We started in her kitchen in West Orange, New Jersey, when I was a teenager. Her lack of measurements confused me as much as my need for measurements irritated her.

"Just do it like I do it," she'd say impatiently.

That was the ever-present message from my Italian-American mother. And to do it like her, or not, played out in the making of the pizza dough.

The day we made pizza together for the first time, she wore a cotton printed housedress typical of the 1950s, covered by a full apron. The pockets of the apron were filled, as usual, with the odds and ends she'd picked up around the house that day: safety pins, a tube of Vaseline, matches, a crumpled grocery list, a handkerchief, teething medicine. Diaper pins were pinned to the top of her apron. Even in a cheap, cotton housedress, my mother could look stylish. She moved her body with confidence as though her footprints belonged on this earth. She was a beautiful woman with thick dark hair, a wide mouth, full lips, straight nose and olive skin that was almost wrinkle free into her 90s. Mom's hair grayed naturally, slowly over the years with streaks as white as salt.

In her usual hurried way, she showed me how to make the dough. She made a small mountain of flour on her wooden cutting board; used her hand to carve a hole in the middle of it; cracked two eggs into the hole; added yeast that had been soaked in hot water (but not too hot); added some olive oil; and kneaded it until all the flour was incorporated into the liquid.

She worked too fast. I was too annoyed and intimidated. I gave up.

Mom's pizza was always good, crusty on the bottom but soft and chewy inside. She baked her pizzas in the top of an old movie film can, 14 inches in diameter by 2 inches deep.

"Is your mom making pizza?" friends would ask when they dropped in. Everyone loved her pizza.

I tried again in my mother's kitchen in Houston, Texas, while I was in college. I gave up again for the same reasons.

Mom on her First Communion Day, 1922

When I had my own kitchen in California, as an adult and mother, I experimented with different pizza recipes until I found one that worked for me. I was happy. People loved it. Friends asked: "Are you making pizza tonight?" I became as famous in my circle as my mom was in hers for pizza making.

When she came to visit me, we tried again with the mountain and the hole. Being in my own kitchen, having made pizza my own way had changed something in me. I wasn't confused. I wasn't intimidated using her method. We worked together, letting the flour fly and splashing the olive oil directly from the bottle.

I put the pizza in the oven. The kitchen smelled of freshly baked bread

Mom, 1922

and simmering tomato sauce. Mom put on the tea, and we sat down to revel in our accomplishment: the master pizza maker and her successful apprentice. She was handing me the baton, and I was solidly taking it. Mother and daughter together.

Two weeks after she left, I received a package from her in the mail. It was her pizza pan, the same movie film can she'd used for nearly 50 years, blackened from all those years of use.

🌱🌱🌱🌱🌱

I will never forget the luscious taste of my mother's ravioli, the dough thin and tender, surrounding a creamy ricotta cheese blended with herbs and floating in a light tomato sauce. As a child, I was given the job of sealing the ricotta cheese mixture snugly inside the rolled out dough. I used a fork and pressed all around each ravioli. Then I'd place the ravioli on a clean sheet spread over the dining room table. It was very labor intensive, but with six kids there were always enough hands.

During one of her visits to California, not long after the pizza extravaganza, we decided to make ravioli. We started as usual with a mound of flour on my wooden cutting board and the hole in the middle. Into the hole went eggs, olive oil, salt and warm water. Using a fork, Mom beat the eggs, oil and water right on the board and slowly added the flour from the edges of the surrounding mountain. When most of the flour was incorporated, she kneaded the dough. I watched carefully and took notes. My dad napped in the living room.

"Don't forget, you can't handle the dough too much or it will be tough," she said while kneading with expert hands.

She rolled the dough into a ball and coated it with olive oil and left it to "rest" while we mixed the ricotta cheese with a handful each of chopped parsley and Parmesan cheese, an egg, and salt and pepper.

"This will fill 38 ravioli," she said. I started to divide that by how many people we were and, as usual, I worried that we hadn't made enough. My mom always said, "You didn't make enough if you don't have leftovers." Because of this, I always overdo it. My husband, Roger, says I cook for an army.

We rolled the dough into long, thin strips four inches wide and put a heaping tablespoon of the ricotta mixture every four inches. Then covered it sandwich style with another strip of dough, cut between the mounds of cheese and used a fork to secure the tiny packages.

"Prick two small holes in each ravioli," she instructed using a toothpick. "They have to be placed very gently in the boiling water."

Before cooking them, we sat down to admire our work. My dad walked into the kitchen, inspected the ravioli and nodded his approval. "It's time for a glass of wine," he announced.

"You have a well equipped kitchen," my mother said. I felt like I'd passed a test, like finally I was a grown up.

🍅🍅🍅🍅🍅

My Mom married into a well known, well educated Italian American family in Newark, the Castellano family. My grandfather was City Attorney, and my Uncle Nick, my father's brother, was Chief Magistrate of the city of Newark. My parents married on May 30, 1939, and had six children: Mary Jo Castellano San Giacomo, Lorrie Castellano (that's me), Mena Castellano Scialli, Michele Castellano Senac, Regina Castellano and Joe Castellano.

Growing Up with My Italian-American Mother

When I think of growing up with my first-generation immigrant mother, her fear of being labeled a "gavone" is the first thing that comes to my mind. "Gavone" is southern Italian dialect for low class, uneducated, uncouth. It was a description of people who, in my mother's eyes, wore flashy clothes, heavy, fake, gold chains, talked loudly, and spoke with a Newark accent. My mom had a fear of being labeled a low class Italian, and she worked ceaselessly to wipe out any trace of that in her or her children.

When I was 12 years old, I came home from school, excited about the prospect of my friends and me forming a gang. It was popular for each gang member to wear identical jackets in colorful satins with the name of the gang embroidered on the back. I had my eyes set on pink satin. Naively, I told my mother about it.

Mom on her honeymoon, 1939

"Che scorn! Madonna mia! Mannagia! Geeda bought-sonna!" My mother streamed out this indecipherable dialect. I never knew the translation, but I did know the meaning. "Shame on you! How could you even think a thing like that?"

I can still see her hands flying, her face fierce, her voice loud and disapproving. She was determined to protect her family from being gavone so she began planning our escape from Newark that very night. The next year we were safely housed in West Orange, a very respectable suburb of Newark, far from the gavones who formed gangs, wore pink satin, talked loudly, and, in my mother's view, had the wrong kind of fun.

Not being a gavone took a lot of her energies and therefore, mine. Keeping my exuberance in check was a full time job, and I usually failed at it. When I read Maria Laurino's book *Were You Always an Italian,* I realized I was a Versace in a household that aspired to be Armani. My tastes were big and bold as were Versace-designed clothes, not sedate and classic like Giorgio Armani. But I tried because being a gavone enraged my mother.

My parents bought a summer house in Lake George, New York, just before we moved to West Orange. This was another of my mother's plans to keep us away from the gavones at the Jersey Shore. The Jersey Shore was a dangerous place in her eyes, full of girls who teased their hair, wore heavy makeup and tight pants and did all the catastrophic things that could happen because of the tight pants.

Her children were safe at last.

The War of Two Cultures

Mom and Dad at Bud Lake, New Jersey, July 21, 1935

My mother was a complicated, conflicted woman. In her were two cultures warring for dominance. One side of my mother was a Mama Del Sud as described by Maria Laurino in *Old World Daughter, New World Mother*. She was "fiercely protective, terribly fearful, histrionic and utterly devoted" to her children. She believed in self sacrifice. She was suspicious of independence, in fact, saw independence as a betrayal of her and the family. She was loyal to a rigid code of conduct, worried about what others thought, insisted on duty and respect.

The other side of my mother was her desire to be American, to shake off the yoke of that hyphenated part of her. She wanted to feed and enhance in her and her children the independent, upwardly mobile, unattached, unburdened attitude of Americans.

These two warring sides played out in our daily life.

When we lived in West Orange, we had a next door neighbor who was a well educated young woman in her early 30s. She lived with her Italian-American parents and worked in New York City. She commuted to her job and passed our house on the way to the train station daily. She was always dressed in soft wool classic suits, stockings, heels, muted scarves, and leather gloves. She was the perfect image of what in the 1950s was a "career girl." The women in my family were either wives and mothers or aspired to be and were just working until Mr. Right, who was Italian-American, of course, came along. Our neighbor, the Career Girl, may have been doing the same

Mom and Dad, Mary Jo, Mena and Lorrie, 1945

thing, but from afar she looked independent, important and had lots of money for beautiful clothes. I wanted to be just like her.

"See what all that independence gets you," my mom would say whenever I mentioned her. "She can't even find a nice husband."

"But she's a career girl!" I answered with enthusiasm.

"Don't get any ideas," she'd warn, raising her voice.

The message was clear. Don't even think about it. It's dangerous and hurts your chances of getting married and joining, as an adult, the tight-knit group of women in the family.

The message was also unclear because of the push she always gave me to get good grades, go to a good college, and be successful in a good career.

My independence was seen through this confusing, fear-coated lens.

"Oh, Miss Independent," my mother would spit out disparagingly, as I walked out the door to meet friends. I was the inconsiderate, traitorous daughter, choosing an outsider over family. She could have said "after all I've done for you." She didn't, but I got the message. I was the ungrateful daughter refusing to sacrifice what I wanted for the sake of the family.

It was a struggle for my mother to let go of any of her children. Some of her devotion was sweet and loving, like when I left for college, she wrote to me every day, never missing a day. My father, also, sent me a note with a $5 bill in it every week, never failing. My mother contacted an old family friend and her husband, both Italian-Americans, who lived in Baltimore. They swung into action, becoming surrogate parents to me. I always knew I had a place at their dinner table. Even when I didn't want one.

Mom, Dad and Mary Jo, Mena, Michele and Lorrie, 1953

After I graduated from college, a friend asked me to share an apartment with her for the summer. The apartment was a 15-minute drive from my parent's house. I was delighted because it meant some independence and a chance to spread my wings. Not to mention meeting the cute boys who hung around the apartment pool!

"Why do you want to do that when you have a perfectly good room right here in this house?" my father complained. He had a way of looking so disappointed and shaking his head from side to side as if to say, "I don't know what you're thinking, but it's all wrong."

"Don't get any ideas," my mother chimed in with her usual refrain.

It was as though wanting independence at 22 was doing something irretrievably wrong, that I'd hurt them beyond redemption. The guilt I felt displayed itself in a deep blush of embarrassment and then anger. I went to my room to regroup. After a short time, I patiently explained my reasons, emphasized it was just for two months and promised to return home in September. They reluctantly agreed. The guilt was still with me, as was the fear that I was doing something terribly wrong, but I pretended extreme confidence and moved out. It worked. And I did have fun flirting with the boys by the pool!

As I negotiated this mine field towards incremental independence, I realized the war my mother fought her whole life was now inside me. The struggle was in building an independent life while enjoying the safety and comfort of our large Italian-American family. Clinging to family, suspicion of outsiders may have been functional when living on the edge of survival in 19th century southern Italy. Mal'occhio, the evil eye, may have been a good substitute for protection in the absence of education and modern medicine. But in American society, these old values can be like molasses, persistently sticky and hard to get away from. It's also sweet and guarantees you a place at the table. That's the legacy of Italian Americans. The trick is to navigate to get the best of both worlds. Our parents struggled with this their whole lives, and we, their children, did as well.

Parenting by Aphorism

My mother parented by aphorism, the fast and furious parenting technique: say as little as possible, as loud as possible and don't worry about the contradictions.

"You've missed the boat," she'd yell, raising her hands to indicate disaster and hopelessness. Her declaration would leave me panicky. It had such a finality to it. The boat was gone forever and I was left behind. It took years to realize that opportunities come more than once.

"You either get married or be a nun," was the advice I received when trying to create a future for myself.

"If things could be done twice, they'd be done right." At least that had some hope in it. Of course, it also assumed I failed the first time around.

"The only thing that can't be fixed is death," she'd declare with as much certainty as "you've missed the boat."

My Fast and Furious Mom

My parents' youngest child, my brother Joe, was 13 years old when two of Uncle Mike's sons came to live in our house after Uncle Mike died. They were the last of a string of relatives who used our home as a refuge. Ours was the house anyone who was unemployed came to live in until they found another job and "got back on their feet." Aunt Eleanore and our two cousins, Roberta and Kenny, lived with us while their father was in the Marines during World War II. My father's mother, Grandma Castellano, and his sister, Aunt Mena, lived with us for a while. My mom and dad were the people everyone, family and friends, went to with problems to be solved. Somehow, even with six and then eight children, my mom managed everything. And she made it all seem easy. Everything looked effortless, but underneath she was juggling, arranging, organizing, problem solving, cooking, cleaning, making sure there were enough beds, linens, towels, food in the house, that our homework got done, that we followed the rules, that we kept to the budget. She drove everyone in the family to doctor's appointments. She helped care for her sick mother until Grandma Cibella died.

She never sat down. She never expressed exhaustion. But she was overwhelmed. The task she had and the number of people she took care of was Herculean. Her frustrations came out, not in tears or cries for help but in migraine headaches and persistent anger.

Mom had a temper that could erupt explosively in a split second. "What mood is she in today?" we kids asked each other while tiptoeing around the house. What kind of mood I'd meet when I came home from school was always on my mind. Our task of keeping her from getting angry and making her happy was also Herculean. She was a yeller and a screamer. She didn't hit. The only thing she threw were words. She'd fling them at us with such force, we'd be paralyzed into speechlessness. Her angry words took ours away. She expected us children to think as she did:

"Didn't you notice the dishes in the sink?" she'd yell as she walked in the door. "Couldn't you think to wash them?" her voice getting even louder.

"We were playing," we'd say guiltily. And slink away towards the kitchen sink, our playing turning sour in our stomachs.

Mom in the Kitchen

The only time I saw my mother carefree was while cooking in the kitchen. There was a freedom in her cooking, a careless, lightheartedness that was not present in the rest of her life. She was an inventive, creative cook. She improvised and never held herself accountable to a recipe. She was the queen of "make do."

"If you're missing an ingredient," she'd shrug, "substitute what you have."

When friends dropped by unexpectedly, she'd go to a refrigerator that looked empty to me and she'd pull together a delicious meal with great ease. She was fast.

She did everything fast. Like dinner:

My father expected dinner as soon as he got home, and it was usually ready. On the rare occasion when it wasn't, she had a few tricks up her sleeve which she taught me.

"If dinner isn't ready when your husband comes home, set the table. He'll think it won't be long."

"If dinner is going to be late, fry up some garlic. The house will smell like you've been cooking all day."

Having dinner as a family every night was one of the best traditions I learned from my parents. We ate together every night. And every night it was a home-cooked meal. We didn't answer the phone or the doorbell during this family time.

My mom packed our lunch for school every morning. She always said you can make anything into a sandwich, and I can attest that she lived by that code. How I longed for bologna sandwiches when I was in the high school cafeteria. Instead, I was struggling with pepper and egg sandwiches, broccoli rabe or stuffed cherry peppers between two pieces of thick Italian bread. I had a hard time managing the dripping olive oil while imagining every boy watching me and laughing.

"Stunod. Gee la walla zen! Don't say such a stupid thing," was her response when I asked for a "normal" sandwich. "Those boys only wish they could have your lunch."

She was right. All our friends flocked to our house after school. They'd tease us that we were not allowed to drink soda and only offered them orange juice. But they never refused.

My Uncle Nick, the Judge, was popular with my friends. Sometimes when they'd come over, they'd pull my father aside.

"Mr. Castellano," they'd ask my father timidly, "Do you think the Judge could fix this speeding ticket for me?"

My father would let them squirm a while. The Judge always agreed. It probably wasn't the orange juice they came for after all.

The Fashionable Girls

My mom survived what seemed like an onslaught of family responsibility by keeping a tight circle of women friends around her. They called themselves "The Fashionable Girls." They saw each other regularly but, more importantly, they talked on the phone constantly. It was good company and support for my Mom, and she laughed a lot while with them. There were seven "Fashionable Girls" and with their husbands, all from the old neighborhood, they had riotous parties. I'd sit at the top of the stairs when it was at our house and listen to them talk, joke and tease one another.

My mother was surrounded by a large extended family and a close group of friends, but all of that changed in 1961.

History Repeats Itself

Standard Oil of New Jersey merged with Humble Oil in 1961, and my father's job was transferred from New York City to Houston, Texas. Our whole family moved, except my oldest sister, Mary Jo, who was married. My father's fear of not getting another job at age 49 played a big role. To move was an extraordinary decision on their part.

Mom at a garden party, circa 1940

Leaving New Jersey in 1961 was a smaller version of what my mom's parents had done in 1903, leaving Caposele, Italy. Texas, like Caposele, was far away; plane travel was unusual and expensive at the time; the culture was foreign. They did speak English in Texas but just barely. My parents planned the move carefully, one step at a time, just like Tomaso and Camille Cibella before them. And they missed their homeland, New Jersey. We all missed the extended family that had always surrounded us. The number around our table was reduced to seven. And then two more were added when our cousins, Michael and Eddie Castellano, came to live with us. We missed the easy-to-get Italian ingredients for the food we loved. Grandpa Cibella sent us "care packages" filled with loaves of Giordano's Italian bread. My mother wrapped them in tin foil and kept them in the refrigerator to keep them fresh for as long as possible. We all felt we were in a foreign land.

Moving away was traumatic for all of us. We were adrift in a strange place. The heat was unbearable. When you walked outside, it hit you like a wall. It was breathtaking. And the bugs were giant things, two-inch-long roaches with wings and other strange, prehistoric looking creatures. We had to have our house fumigated every three months. We were in tropical heat and everything proliferated.

We didn't know where we belonged. In Texas, we were from New Jersey, and in New Jersey, we were from Texas. Our wardrobes changed. The heavy winter clothes were stored. We bought sun dresses in light colors and sandals to wear all year around. Texas women were a different breed. No self sacrifice here! They cared for themselves, sparing no expense. They were lacquered, polished, shaved, coifed, and white. Mom's migraines increased. She was often in bed in a darkened room for a whole day. Her irritability and anger did not stay in New Jersey. It moved with us and increased.

Mom and Dad, 1960

Dad took it in stride. He moved with his cohorts and was now carpooling with them. So he had the familiarity of his job as well as a raise and promotion. With no snow to shovel, no relatives to step in and save at a moment's notice, life was easier for him. More disposable income meant a housekeeper and more meals out. We slowly adjusted. Even Mom.

Many companies were moving to the Southwest at that time. My parents found some other Italian-American transplants and even made new friends who were not Italian- Americans. With two small children in school, they got involved in their classrooms, the church and with the neighbors. Before long they had friends, and the house was full again. My father started playing golf; my mother joined a gym and started swimming.

The world got bigger. It became acceptable to date someone who wasn't Italian-American. We learned that we all loved Mexican food. Cold beers sometimes replaced red wine. New Jersey was still the Homeland, but we joked that Houston had become the family Corporate Headquarters.

But some things never changed. When I left home to get a master's degree at UC, Berkeley, my father gave me a key to the front door and said, "you're always welcome back, any time." But Mom, true to her Mama del Sud self, sent me information about Catholic Women's Retreats in Berkeley and articles about San Francisco and its high suicide rate due to estrangement from family. I managed to survive the separation.

She managed to learn that our relationship could thrive even with distance.

When my father died in 1996, my mom insisted on moving back to New Jersey. She bought a house five doors down from her sister, Eleanore, and lived there until she died in 2011 at age 96.

My mother remained feisty her whole life. Even at the age of 90, she fired her caregiver without telling any of her children saying, "I just didn't want her around."

For her 90th birthday, instead of the customary big party, she requested a gathering of only her children, leaving spouses and grandchildren out. She was still Mama del Sud surrounding herself with her children. We congregated in her small townhouse, sleeping on blow up mattresses and couches, getting up in the morning to put the "gravy" on. The house once again smelled of meatballs, braciole and sausage simmering in tomatoes. We found Dad's old tapes of Frank Sinatra, Louis Prima and Jimmy Durante. We sang as we cooked, chopping and stirring and tasting, preparing a feast for our mother on her 90th birthday. The house was full of flowers. Her nieces, nephews and friends, who had turned to her for comfort and advice, remembered her with bouquets, cards and gifts.

Her advice to the women in our family had been to remind them of their value and to pick men who were worthy of them.

"You are the Queen of Sheba," she'd say. "And don't you forget it!" she added in case we weren't listening.

So we presented her with her own crown and hailed her as the Queen Mother. She waved us off as if to say, "don't make such a fuss." But she was pleased. My mother looked beautiful. She was always a stylish dresser even when our budget didn't allow for much. Now she wore her black pants and white v-neck sweater regally, the tiny gold heart from my father at her throat. A short strand of white crystals, elegant and understated, around her neck. Her hair, pure white and soft, framed her almost wrinkle-free face. We popped champagne, toasting our mother. She was happy. We were there, all her children, safe with her. And she was proud – all her children were thriving – independent with families and lives of their own but enjoying being in a big Italian- American family and being close to each other, relying on each other, loving each other. No one became a nun, everyone married. She'd done her job. The next time we were all together was at her 2011 memorial service.

Mom and Dad's wedding day, 1939.
First row, left to right: Aunt Dolly, Aunt Eleanore, Mom, and friend Dolly.
Back row, left to right: Uncle Nick, Uncle Mike, Grandpa Castellano,
Dad and Uncle Kenny.

A Word about Italian dialect

My mother always said she spoke low class or uneducated Italian. It took me years to realize that the language Tomaso and Camille spoke and taught their children was a dialect. It was a spoken language, not a written one, so spelling is not important. It was inflection that said it all. Words were not wasted on the positive or on people or actions you thought highly of. They were saved and used freely for belittling jabs, anger, snap judgments, criticism and despair. They were most often spit out like a bitter taste in the mouth. You didn't have to know the meaning of the words to know the sentiment hurled your way.

Mom in Palo Alto, California, 1995

Here are a few of the Italian dialect words and terms that were spoken frequently by our mother and her family, along with the interpretation.

Stunod – this was a term used many times to tag someone who wasn't thinking, who did something stupid or thoughtless, as in, "You're stunod" or "He's a stunod" or, worst of all, "Are you stunod?" (*stonato* in standard Italian)

Gabbadotz – refusal to change your mind, stubborn, hard-headed, as in, "You're gabbadotz." (*testa dura* in standard Italian)

Mooshamoos – slow in getting work done, not working efficiently, unresponsive, as in, "You're so mooshamoos."

Squistamod – dirty, unkempt person, slovenly in personal dress, as in, "He's a squistamod."

Mamaluch – someone who is soft in the head, who doesn't think straight, as in, "Don't be a mamaluch."

Gedrool – stupid or silly, as in, "What a gedrool."

Pacenzia – patience. My mother used this word often, especially when we children did something that annoyed her. She would say out loud, "Pacenzia."

Dad: Joseph "Joe" John Castellano

(8/12/1912 – 1/31/1996)

Dad as a baby, circa 1913

My dad was a gentle man, short and trim, impeccably dressed and always with a white handkerchief in his pocket. I ironed those handkerchiefs when I was growing up. He always had a clean stack of them in his dresser drawer. He had a head of thick, black, wavy hair which he parted in the middle. He wore 1940s style wire-rim glasses. He had deep dimples when he smiled.

He was a taciturn man. It was uncomfortable for him to speak up for himself. Decision-making was particularly hard for him. He worried about making the wrong choice, as if every decision was monumental and could lead to irreversible mistakes. He was concerned about stepping out of line, being found ill prepared. You could tell how much fear and uncertainty he had to overcome by the amount of annoyance and irritation in his voice when a problem came up. He wanted a simple life. But he had a large extended family to guide and six children to raise. A simple life never came to him. He was the responsible one for the entire family. He pushed through his reserve and guardedness all his life, and it was not easy. But he did it.

He worked for Standard Oil of New Jersey for 38 years. A loyal employee from 1937, he moved with the company to Houston, Texas, in 1962.

"In order to get that job, I had to change my name. They just wouldn't hire an Italian in 1937. So I dropped the o from Castellano," he chuckled at the daringness of it, "and applied under the French name." Here he used air quotes so I'd get the picture, "Castellane."

"After I was there for a few months, I went to Personnel and told them they'd misspelled my name, and they just corrected it, no questions asked. That's how I got my job."

He started in the Marine Division in Payroll and went to Pace University at night to study accounting. During the war, in the dead of night, he secretly ferried out payroll to the oil tankers in New York Harbor. He climbed up the sides of those big ships and handed the strong box to the Captain. He did his duty, although clandestine work was way outside his comfort level. His only regret during that time, he told me, was missing dinner with his wife and children.

Mom and Dad were a good team. She was fearless and ambitious. They had a shared vision for the family, and he needed the push she often gave him. They worked well together.

"I got L'ubrem" is what my mother often said when speaking about my Dad. He was "the prize." To her there was no one who could compare. They grew up in the same neighborhood and "kept company" for seven years before they married. My father's good friend and parish priest, Father Artioli, accompanied them on almost all their dates. That's why it took so long.

Dad with Grandma Castellano, 1940

They married on May 30, 1939. They had six children: Mary Jo Castellano San Giacomo, born 8/26/40; Loretta "Lorrie" Castellano, born 2/10/42; Mena Castellano Scialli, born 1/19/44; Michele Castellano Senac, born 1/14/47; Regina "Gina" Castellano, born 10/23/54; and Joseph "Joe" Castellano, born 12/29/56. Their marriage lasted 67 years until my father died in 1996 at age 84.

My dad was a family man, and the heart of the family was dinner each night promptly at 5:30. I got my political education at that dinner table. We talked about city politics and national elections and the Democratic Party. He was a staunch Democrat and thinking of him "rolling over in his grave" keeps me loyal to this day. The dinner table is also where we heard the family news and, if we stayed real quiet, the family gossip as well. Most of our values about looking out for people, giving what we could to help others, came from discussions at the dinner table.

"I talked to Dolly today. Her marriage is in shambles," Mom informed Dad about his sister one night at dinner.

"That sister of mine," he said shaking his head from side to side. "She never listens. I told her not to marry him. And why she had to have Mama move in with them is beyond me."

Mom and Dad on their honeymoon   *Dad with Lorrie, 1942*

He was expected to solve a lot of problems. You'd hear the exasperation in his voice. He'd reach for his Camels, light up, take a deep drag, raise his head to the ceiling and blow the smoke out in a long forceful stream. You could tell he would have been happier sitting in his favorite chair reading his *Newark Evening News*. He just wanted some peace and quiet.

"Now where is Mama going to live?" he asked, knowing full well what the answer would be.

We bought a single bed, and Grandma moved into the baby's room.

When report cards came home, he went through them line by line. Comportment was as important to him as grades. He helped us with our homework every night. We tried what little patience he had.

"Gabbadotz," hard head, he'd say, reaching in his shirt pocket for his cigarettes, shaking his head and trying to calm himself.

"What's wrong with you?" Counting on our fingers infuriated him. He just couldn't understand how an accountant's child could have so much trouble with simple math.

My dad did what he thought was the responsible thing at all times. He followed the rules. He accepted the family's code of behavior, the authority of the Catholic Church, the U.S. Government, and the Democratic Party.

During my first year at Berkeley, I came home for winter break sporting a peace button. It was the height of the Vietnam War. We sat around the dinner table as I described being tear gassed in anti-war demonstrations. I was critical of the policy of the government and the reaction of the police. I must admit I enjoyed the reaction I was getting. My nonconformist point of view allowed me to seem more grown up than I actually felt inside.

My father was so exasperated with my heretical views, his hand automatically reached in his shirt pocket for his cigarettes, only to remember he'd given up smoking a year before. He shook his head as if all his guidance had been for nothing, and I was a traitor to all the values he held dear. Finally, he invoked his fall-back philosophy which I'd heard all my life,

"You can't fight City Hall," was his angry response. Then he shrugged in resignation over the lost cause I'd become. Fighting City Hall was exactly what I was doing.

He was fearful for me. He would have liked me to stay safe in the sanctuary of the Church, the refuge of the family and the stronghold of the U.S. Government. To him it wasn't safe to have a difference of opinion with such powerful institutions. But his resignation and fear was also his understanding that his values were not enough to keep me safe in a 1960s world.

"What are you gunna do?" he said, giving up. With that the discussion ended.

Having different views and asserting independence had its price in my family, and seeing my father so distressed and defeated by my non-conformist views was a big price to pay.

As tentative as he was outside the family, within the family he knew how to get a party going. He loved music. He would play his ukulele for us, wearing a hat with a turned-up rim and always had a new tape of the old songs for us to listen to. Asti Spumante was his preferred celebration drink. He loved it and would put it on ice before any family celebration. We never let on that we preferred champagne and always toasted with his Asti after the cork popped. He'd slip in his latest tape and move the furniture aside so we could dance.

Two steps forward. One step back. We learned to dance as children on my father's feet. He'd waltz us around the room to the romantic music of Old Blue Eyes, his favorite, Frank Sinatra. We knew all the words, even as little kids.

It was New Year's Eve, 1971. The whole family and a scattering of friends are at my sister Gina's house. All the lights in the house are blazing. Candles are burning. Christmas tree lights are blinking. The music is on, and we're singing, our hands in a fist to mimic a microphone. Gina has an idea. She passes out tablespoons, and they instantly become the family mic and a necessary party prop.

Dad jumps in with a Rockette kicking routine, a daughter on each side, and then the line lengthens with all of his children kicking in unison and singing, laughing so hard, we're holding on to each other to stay upright.

"Don't let the Castellano kids get near the spoons," our friends tease.

One time during the party, I saw my dad standing off to the side just watching all of us with a small, satisfied smile on his face. He loved seeing us all together, enjoying ourselves. Dad taught us all how to have fun. He was a good antidote to my mother's no-nonsense attitude.

ಆ ಆ ಆ ಆ ಆ

When Dad retired at 63, he took over the making of the tomato sauce on Sunday morning. Like his mother before her, Mom still served some form of macaroni every Sunday, Tuesday and Thursday. He'd been eating this way his whole life, and it upset him greatly to be surprised by anything else on those days. He took making the tomato sauce very seriously, and he perfected his meatballs to taste exactly like his mother's. My sister Gina learned the recipe from him. The only difference is that she bakes the meatballs instead of frying them, a very slight nod to our fat-free frenzied world.

Dad and Mom enjoying a private moment, 1989

ಆ ಆ ಆ ಆ ಆ

After I moved to California, I spoke to my Dad on the phone once a week. Before I hung up each time I'd say to him, "I love you." His response was always, "Okay."

After a few years of this, I thought it was time I teach him to say 'I love you' back. So on the next phone call, I started my lesson.

"Dad, when I say 'I love you' to you, I want you to say 'I love you' back."

"Oh, you know I do."

"But I want you to say it."

"You're becoming a crazy Californian."

"No, no, say it."

"okIloveyoulorrie."

"No, Dad," I said in an exaggerated tone, "say it like you mean it."

"Iloveyoulorrie."

Say it like this and I stretched out each word in a sing song fashion that got him chuckling.

He repeated magnifying every word, "I Luuve Yoo Lorrrrrrrie."

"That's good," I encouraged. "Now say it whenever we talk, okay?"

"Okay," he said with mock resignation. And he did.

Dad in his easy chair, 1987

Dad was in Intensive Care. Tubes and wires snaked from his body to incomprehensible machines. He was swollen and pale. His deep dimples gone. It was unclear how conscious he was. He hadn't spoken a word since he came out of surgery many hours before. My mom was at his side. All of his children were in the waiting room hoping for his recovery, uncertain what would happen.

We'd decided that we would each have a little time alone with him. I went first. My mother was about to leave the room as I walked in. Before she left, she leaned down close to my father's face.

"Now, Joe," she said sternly, "when the children talk to you, you answer them." He was barely conscious, and my mother was still prodding him.

When I told my father I loved him for the last time that day in the hospital, he moved his lips but no sound came out. I want to believe he said "I love you too," but that could be wishful thinking that he heard me and could respond. Or it could be that my mother's admonition had roused him to give his child his last bit of strength.

At my father's memorial, I introduced myself to one of his friends, telling him I was Joe's daughter from California. "Oh," he said, "Joe told me about you and how you taught him to say 'I love you.' We had a good laugh over that." A warm feeling spread through me. My father had enjoyed my instruction and even told his friend about it. When I heard that, I missed him more than ever.

LaFest' (dialect for The Festival)
Caposele, Italy, and Newark, New Jersey

We left Gerardo and Josephina's carrying sausage, cheeses, bread and olives.

We drove up the hill just outside Caposele following the faded wooden signs that pointed the way to Monastery Materdomini, looking for the church my mother had told me about my whole childhood. I was expecting a tiny stone church. In my imagination I would enter under a low stone arch and through a heavy wooden door to find an altar covered in tiny candles and sweet smelling flowers. The pews would be worn to a shine, and the windows would let in lovely filtered sunlight through stained glass. I expected to see clothed statues of saints and old ladies in black praying. But it was nothing like that. The 1980 earthquake had destroyed the tiny structure, and what replaced it was more like a giant A-frame than a church. The building looked like someone's idea of what a modern structure should look like, that someone never having seen any good contemporary architecture. We walked in through heavy glass doors. It was cavernous with an attempt at an updated version of stained glass windows. I thought the townspeople must be proud to have this "modern" tribute to their favorite saint. To me, it was such a disappointment. I longed for the chapel of my imagination.

We wandered around. I was looking for the register where my grandparents' marriage was recorded. I never found it, but in a small, dark alcove, I found St. Gerard. Not his statue but his body laid out in a glass coffin. I'd seen relics my whole life, bits of bone and flesh and hair set in tiny gold filigree lockets. But this was the entire body. It conjured up the macabre mysteries of the Catholic Church: revengeful Satan, exorcism, punishing hell and secret enigmatic rites, all the black magic which drove me from the Church. The same religion that gave my grandparents strength and hope left me with the feeling it was all primitive superstition. I lingered, thinking of my own journey from the Catholic school girl I was. Then I reached for my husband Roger's hand and suggested a glass of wine. On the way out we saw relics of another kind, the bones of the old church, moss covered stones, hand chiseled, scattered and waiting.

We wandered down the hill through a forest of pine and found a small restaurant. The wine was homemade and delicious. We ordered pasta con pomodoro.

As we ate I noticed well worn decorations of paper and tinsel on either side of the street.

"What celebration did we miss?" I asked the owner who spoke a remnant of English.

"Santo Gerardo," he smiled.

Of course. It was October, the month the Italians in Caposele and in Newark, New Jersey, paid homage to their patron saint, Gerardo Maiella. Santo Gerardo was born in 1726 and worked tirelessly among the poor of Avellino Province. It was a custom to pray to Santo Gerardo for easy childbirth or in cases of difficulty conceiving. The men of Newark commissioned a statue of him from Italy and formed the Society of San Gerardo. They were the ones who managed the annual feast, known as LaFest'.

All thoughts of black magic and demonic sorcery left me, and I began telling Roger about this charmed part of my childhood.

"Every October 16th we'd go to La Fest,' the festival of Saint Gerard," I said excitedly.

"It was held in front of St. Lucy's Church and spilled out to all the streets in the neighborhood. We'd always go at night. To me that night was magical." My hands were starting to talk for me.

"Four tiered arches of multi colored lights were strung from one side of the street to the other. Oh, you should have seen it!" I got excited just remembering that night.

"The street was closed to traffic and crowded with people. Women in black would be sitting at their windows waiting for the saint to come by. Small altars were erected on many of the front steps of the houses, and they were decorated with candles, flowers and ribbons."

I took a sip of wine. I was no longer sitting with Roger. I was back in the Little Italy of my childhood.

"The highlight of LaFest' was the carrying of the statue of Santo Gerardo on a wooden pallet through the streets. My grandfather was one of the guards of honor. We'd cheer when we saw him. The strain of such a heavy load showed on my Grandpa's face. It's a wonder the statue didn't topple. So many people would run after the saint and pull on his cloak to pin money on it. I'd never seen so much money in my life. The whole cloak was covered in bills of different denominations.

"Behind the statue women would walk holding big candles. Sometimes the candle was as tall as the person carrying it. There were also people walking barefoot in supplication or thanksgiving. Seeing those candles burning and the praying, barefoot men and women added a mysterious aura to the night."

I was silent for a while because talking about it raised in me the same strange primitive feelings I had back then. And it wasn't the first time that had happened. I thought of that festival when I studied Macbeth, the dark castle and bloodied hands of

Lady Macbeth or discovered Jan Brueghel paintings. The festival had an ancient pagan quality to it. I stopped to make sure Roger knew what I meant. He did, but I added, "Like a time before science."

The pasta con pomodoro was served. Comfort food. Just what I needed. Roger poured more wine. The family who owned the restaurant looked on. The cook stood with one hand holding the other in front of his ample body.

The pasta was homemade. Not al dente. I thought my father would love this. I continued.

"And oh, the food, Roger," I said.

"Both sides of the street were crowded with small concession stands that sold Italian food cooked by the restaurants in the neighborhood." The thought of that food was almost overwhelming. It sent an army of memories and feelings marching through me.

"Sausage and peppers sandwiches. Bite-size pieces of spicy sausage sautéed with thin slices of green peppers and lots of onions. The torpedo-shaped rolls," my hands forming them in the air to make sure Roger got the full picture, "were stuffed, hot and dripping with the fat of the sausage and olive oil. It was so messy to eat but so worth it."

Then I remembered the necklaces of roasted hazelnuts.

"There were nuts strung on string that I'd wear around my neck and nibble as we walked. And torrone, a hard glazed candy embedded with nuts. It was so hard that when you told the vendor how much you wanted, he used an ax to chop off just the right size. It stuck to your teeth so the sweetness stayed with you for a long time.

"There were also meatball sandwiches, grilled steak and onions, lemon ice and gelato. There were cheeses wrapped in string and pepperoni hung swinging from the tops of the stalls. Cookies of all kinds stacked in mounds on large round platters. Struffoli, small marble sized deep fried dough drenched in a honey mixture of tangerine peels and vermouth.

"I licked my fingers to get as much honey as I could. But the best and most exotic were the long pieces of sweet dough tied into a big bow, about six inches across." I held my fingers apart in case Roger had forgotten what six inches looked like. "Those bows were deep fried and also doused in honey. Little colored sprinkles decorated them."

We lingered, finishing the wine and watching the sun go down behind the mountains.

As we were leaving, Roger asked for the name of the wine, as he'd enjoyed it so much. The owner looked surprised.

"We make our own," he said still looking puzzled as if to say, "Doesn't everyone?"

❧❧❧❧❧

I went back to La Fest' with my mother in 2002 when she was 87. It had been moved to the new St. Lucy's Church, and it wasn't the same. Food was no longer cooked by neighborhood restaurants. Hot dogs, cotton candy and ice cream sandwiches wrapped in paper replaced all those traditional Italian-American dishes. Balloons and cheap trinkets changed the scene and mood. There was no Little Italy. No Italian ladies looking out their windows to greet Saint Gerard. Everything had changed with urban renewal. Everything was leveled, and the Italian families had scattered to various suburbs. It was too dangerous to parade Santo Gerardo with so much money pinned to his cape. But we saw my grandfather's name on the plaque inside the church as a founding member of the Saint Gerard Society. We lit a candle in his honor.

"Come on, Mom," I said taking her arm. "I'll make you some good sausage and peppers when we get home."

❧❧❧❧❧

In 2010, my sister, Regina and her husband, David Barnhart, went to Caposele. She told me that the hand-cut, moss-covered stones I'd seen when leaving the modern Materdomini were used to reconstruct the small chapel of my Grandparent's wedding within the walls of the modern church. She described my imaginary chapel right down to the tiny candles, sweet smelling flowers and old ladies in black, praying.

*The family comes together for Mom's 90th birthday, 2005.
Left to right: Gina, Mena, Mary Jo, Mom, Lorrie, Michele, Joe.*

Part Two

Recipes and Stories Around the Table
Ricette e Racconati Intorno al Tavolo

Chapter 4

SMALL BITES
Piccoli Morsi

Cannellini Bean Bruschetta

Serves: 4–6

INGREDIENTS:

1 can cannellini beans (19 ounces)

4 tablespoons extra virgin olive oil

3 cloves garlic, chopped

½ teaspoon fresh rosemary or oregano, chopped

¼ teaspoon hot red pepper flakes

Salt and pepper

1 small round French baguette for crostini or crackers

METHOD:

Prepare crostini by slicing baguette in ½-inch rounds and brushing with olive oil. Place on baking sheet in a 375° oven 10–15 minutes or until crostini are light brown.

While crostini are baking, sauté olive oil and garlic over low heat until garlic is soft but not brown, add drained beans, reserving about ¼ cup of the liquid in case needed. Add salt, pepper and simmer for 10 minutes. Add oregano or rosemary and pepper flakes. Remove from heat and mash beans with hand masher until the beans are almost smooth. Add some of the reserved liquid if beans seem dry.

TO SERVE:

Place beans in a small, colorful bowl with spreader or spoon. Garnish with fresh rosemary or oregano. Place bowl on large plate and arrange crostini slices around bowl. Serve alone or an additional appetizer can be added. Add a glass of white or red wine.

Mom's Sweet and Sour Red Peppers

Serves: 4

INGREDIENTS:

4 large red bell peppers, cut into ¾-inch slices

½ cup cider vinegar

2 tablespoons sugar

½ cup bread crumbs

4 tablespoons olive oil

METHOD:

Sauté peppers in olive oil for about 10 minutes or until they are slightly soft but still keep their shape. Remove peppers from the pan and add the rest of the ingredients. Mix well. Return the peppers to the pan, stir and heat through.

TO SERVE:

Serve with chunks of Italian bread or in a sandwich.

This dish was traditionally prepared on Christmas Eve, but occasionally my mother prepared it other than a holiday. My mother and her father, Grandpa Tomaso Cibella, loved hot peppers. Grandpa Cibella attributed his longevity (he died at age 97) to eating hot peppers all his life – the hotter the better!

Lorrie adds: My son, Larry, loves hot, spicy food just like his great grandfather. I often have to put a small bowl of hot pepper flakes at his place at the table.

Mom's Stuffed Hot Cherry Peppers – *Peperoni Ripieni*

Serves: Fills 20 cherry peppers

INGREDIENTS:

20 hot cherry peppers, use jars of peppers already cleaned

2 cups bread crumbs

½ cup raisins, chopped

½ cup crushed tomatoes

¼ cup tomato jelly (optional)

5 cloves minced garlic

2 tablespoons capers

Small handful of pine nuts, chopped

1 handful of green olives, pitted and chopped

1 teaspoon oregano, dried

Small handful of chopped Italian parsley

Salt and pepper to taste

Olive oil, enough to moisten whole mixture

10 canned anchovies, cut in half

METHOD:

Preheat oven to 350°. Mix all ingredients together. Add olive oil last and just enough to hold mixture together. Stuff peppers and place ½ anchovy fillet on top of each. Bake 20 minutes.

TO SERVE:

This is a scrumptious mouthful with a glass of wine or other Piccoli Morsi. They are also delicious for lunch between two slices of Italian bread with a glass of red wine.

Stuffed Mushrooms – *Fungi Ripieni*

Serves: about 6

INGREDIENTS:

25 mushrooms

1 cup bread crumbs

⅓ cup grated Parmesan cheese

2 cloves of garlic, chopped

Small handful of chopped Italian parsley

Olive oil to moisten

Salt and pepper to taste

METHOD:

Preheat oven to 350°. Carefully take out stems from mushrooms and wipe caps. Grease cookie sheet. Mix all remaining ingredients together. Moisten with olive oil so that the mixture holds together. Fill each mushroom, drizzle with olive oil, and place on cookie sheet. Bake for 20 minutes or until bread crumbs are slightly browned on top.

TO SERVE:

Arrange the mushrooms in concentric circles. Garnish with fresh parsley or some edible flowers. This is a great dish to bring to a potluck. It takes very little time to make and looks like you're a gourmet cook.

Variation: Jeremy's Stuffed Mushrooms & Stuffed Peppers

This recipe evolved from one of our Christmas Eve cooking marathons. It may change slightly with each holiday (that inherited Italian gene!), yet these mushrooms and peppers are always delicious.

Serves: 8

INGREDIENTS:

1 large jar of hot cherry peppers in vinegar

1 large jar of sweet cherry peppers in vinegar

16 large mushrooms – remove stems and reserve

1 medium onion

4 cloves garlic

1 eggplant, peeled, cut into small squares

¼ pound lump crab meat or 12 medium raw shrimp, peeled and minced

½ cup Parmesan cheese, grated

¾ cup Italian style bread crumbs

White wine – a splash

Salt and pepper to taste

Red pepper flakes to taste

1 teaspoon oregano, dried

½ teaspoon basil, dried

METHOD:

Rinse hot and sweet cherry peppers, removing caps and discarding. Set aside to drain. Sauté eggplant at low heat until it cooks down to almost a paste. Clean out mushrooms, chop stems, and in a separate pan sauté stems with onion and garlic. Add white wine and simmer. Add salt, pepper, oregano, basil and hot pepper flakes. Add sautéed eggplant and minced shrimp. Heat it all together for a few minutes. Put mixture in bowl and add bread crumbs and mix well. Let it cool and then add Parmesan cheese.

Stuff into peppers and mushrooms. Place in oiled baking dish and dust with bread crumbs and remaining Parmesan cheese. Drizzle with olive oil. Bake covered at 400° for 10 minutes until things start to steam. Uncover and bake until tops are nicely brown.

TO SERVE:

Place on platter. If dry, drizzle a little more olive oil on top. Serve with small slices of Italian bread.

❦ *This is another of my mother's recipes that carried with it no specific amount of ingredients. She always prepared what seemed like a huge bowl of antipasto and she mixed and tasted until she felt satisfied. Even today, when I make it, I do as my mother did, adding in ingredients, tasting, observing how it looks, smells, asking others in the kitchen to taste. Lorrie was able to get exact measurements when she was recreating this dish, but she cautions to keep tasting and adjusting while making it.*

Mom's Antipasto

Serves: 16–20

INGREDIENTS:

1 large eggplant, peeled in stripes and cut into 1-inch cubes

1 head of celery, washed and cut into ½-inch pieces

1 jar artichoke hearts, cut into ½-inch pieces

¼ pound green Sicilian olives, pitted and chopped

3 tablespoons capers

1 large green bell pepper, cut into thin slices and then into bite size pieces

4 roasted red peppers (see recipe) or use a good brand of jarred roasted peppers cut into bite-size pieces

1 teaspoon oregano, dried

Large handful of chopped Italian parsley

Large handful of chopped fresh basil

Olive oil to dress and to sauté eggplant

Salt and pepper to taste

METHOD:

Sauté eggplant cubes in olive oil until the pieces are soft. Eggplant absorbs oil very quickly so be sure to have the olive oil nice and hot before you place the eggplant in and mix it immediately so the oil is evenly distributed. Add more if needed. Place eggplant in a large bowl along with all the other ingredients. Mix well. Taste to adjust seasoning.

TO SERVE:

This is a good holiday antipasto for large groups but can be halved for smaller dinner parties. Leftovers can be kept in the refrigerator for a week or more for a quick, delicious snack. Serve with rounds of French or Italian bread. Stuffed mushrooms and stuffed cherry peppers also make a great accompaniment.

Mom's Roasted Peppers – *Peperoni Arrostiti*

Serves: 6–10 as side dish

INGREDIENTS:

10 red or green bell peppers

2 cups olive oil

3 cloves garlic, chopped

1 teaspoon salt

1 teaspoon pepper

METHOD:

Wash and dry peppers, place on the burners of a gas stove, turning the peppers frequently, until they are brown and blistered. Or, pre-heat broiler and cover a heavy baking sheet with foil. Place peppers on sheet and broil until peppers are brown and blistered, turning frequently, for about 20 minutes. Remove peppers and place in a brown paper bag, seal and cover the bag with a clean kitchen towel until cooled to room temperature. Peel and seed peppers. Cut into ¼-inch strips. Toss in a large bowl with oil, garlic, salt and pepper. Cover and refrigerate for at least 4 hours. Bring to room temperature before serving.

TO SERVE:

Place on small platter or in small bowl with sliced Italian bread or crostini. Can also add to a green salad or a sandwich.

LORRIE'S VARIATION:

You can "doctor" jarred roasted peppers by draining them, slicing them and adding chopped garlic, olive oil and salt. But they never taste as good as the ones you make at home. My brother, Joe, makes great roasted peppers and he, like Mom, makes it seem so easy. In fact I've always teased him that I was going to hire him to do "no-anxiety" cooking lessons for me and my friends. He cooks with such ease and, again like my mom, with whatever is in the refrigerator. Cooking without anxiety is the subject for another book and would be titled, *Cooking Like My Brother*.

Roasted peppers and cheese

As a child, watching my mother make roasted peppers was frightening to me. Because she roasted whole peppers right on the stove, seeing her place peppers on the gas flames was scary. She would use long tongs to turn the peppers, but invariably one or two wouldn't turn exactly right and she'd use her fingers to turn them and end up with small burns. In fact, my mother frequently cut herself accidentally with a knife while chopping and preparing foods. It would scare me to see her fingers burned, or a small cut bleed. She always recovered fast, and made light of every incident, and continued on with what she was doing.

She made at least 20 peppers at a time. When they were roasted, she dressed them with olive oil, garlic, and salt and packed them in jars and refrigerated them. She said, "Let them set for several hours before eating them, if you can resist!" They would keep a week or more that way. She loved having peppers on hand for a quick snack or sandwich. Thinking about eating roasted pepper sandwiches with my mother, both of us with olive oil on our chins and fingers, is a happy memory.

Although Grandma Castellano was known for her soft, succulent meatballs, my sister Mary Jo says that stuffed artichokes were the best dish our grandmother ever made. Grandma was in charge of making this dish for Christmas Eve dinner, though she made it often throughout the year. She was very particular about most things. She was meticulous about her home which was always elegantly decorated and sparkling clean. My father used to tell us that as an adolescent, he and his sister Mena were usually given the task of washing each crystal drop on the dining room chandelier. He hated doing that! While cooking, she was in complete control, so much so that my Aunt Dolly referred to her as "The General." Standing at the kitchen counter, a long, front apron covering her dress, she would tell us, "Choose the best artichokes you can find – ones that are medium size and are heavy. Squeeze each one and if you hear a squeak, you'll know they're fresh. And wash and drain them thoroughly." Using a large spoon, she gently mixed the filling until it was just the right consistency. "Keep tasting to make sure the flavors are right," she advised, "and make sure you stuff each leaf fully, and, of course, do not overcook them." My grandmother prepared artichokes much like she did everything else in her life – with perfection.

Grandma Castellano's Stuffed Artichokes – *Carciofi Ripieni*

Serves: 4

INGREDIENTS:

4 large globe artichokes, washed

¼ cup extra-virgin olive oil plus 2 tablespoons

2½ cups bread crumbs

3 garlic cloves, peeled and minced

½ cup Italian parsley leaves, chopped

1 cup Pecorino cheese, grated

Salt and pepper

Juice of 2 lemons

1 stick salted butter, melted

METHOD:

Cut stems off even with the base and discard. Cut ¼ inch off the top of each artichoke and discard. Remove the tough outer leaves. Using scissors, cut the thorns off the remaining leaves. Fill a large pot of water, add artichokes and parboil them for 5 minutes. Drain upside down in a colander. While cooling, make the filling. Preheat oven to 350°. Heat 2 tablespoons olive oil in sauté pan and brown bread crumbs. Place bread crumbs in large bowl and add garlic and parsley. Add cheese, salt and pepper. Stuff the center of each artichoke, and then stuff each of the rows of leaves. Place on oiled baking sheet and bake for 15 minutes or until outer leaves are soft enough to easily remove. When ready, drizzle butter and sprinkle cheese on top.

TO SERVE:

Serve on colorful platter, garnishing with fresh lemons, quartered. Place lemon/butter dipping sauce in center of platter within easy reach. Sauce can be poured over individual artichoke, or as a dip using the artichoke leaf.

Finocchio, or as it was pronounced in the Italian dialect of my family, "feenuk," was a staple on the Christmas Eve table. My mother served it on her Franciscan "Desert Rose" celery dish, which was a long, narrow dish with pink flowers on the sides. The black or green olives against the white fennel and the pink flowers always looked so pretty. My mother knew how to present food, and it is a skill that my siblings and I have acquired too. This simple condiment is a perfect accompaniment to the sometimes heavy feel of Italian food. The licorice taste of the fennel and the juicy saltiness of the olives are very refreshing.

Fennel and Olives – *Finocchio e Olive*

Serves: 6–8

INGREDIENTS:

1–2 fennel bulbs (depending on number of people)

1–2 cans large black and/or green olives, pitted

METHOD:

Wash fennel, cut stalks and fronds off the bulbs. Set aside. Place fennel bulb on its flat bottom, top side up, and cut in half. Cut each fennel half lengthwise into quarters. Then cut each quarter lengthwise into thin wedges.

TO SERVE:

Arrange on long narrow dish using fronds as garnish. Scatter olives over the fennel. Serve cold.

Rice Balls – *Arancini di Riso*

Serves: Makes about 20 rice balls

INGREDIENTS:

Olive oil

2 cups of risotto, cooked in salted water and cooled

2 large eggs, beaten

1½ cup Italian style bread crumbs

20 ½-inch cubes of mozzarella

½ cup Parmesan cheese, grated

Salt to taste

METHOD:

Heat 3 inches of oil in a heavy frying pan. Stir together the eggs, risotto, Parmesan, and ½ cup of the bread crumbs in a bowl. Use 2 tablespoons of the risotto mixture to form balls about 2 inches in diameter. Insert a cube of mozzarella cheese into the middle of each ball. Using the remaining bread crumbs, roll each ball to coat. Add each ball to the hot oil, turning as needed until they are light brown, about 4 minutes. Transfer to paper towel to drain, season with salt.

TO SERVE:

Stack in a colorful bowl and garnish with a sprig of basil. Serve hot.

Mom's Taralles

Serves: Makes 3 dozen

INGREDIENTS:

3 cups flour

½ cup olive oil

2 tablespoons fennel seeds

1 teaspoon salt

2 tablespoons black pepper

Warm water as needed

METHOD:

Preheat oven to 400°. Lightly grease baking sheet. Bring pot of water to a boil on the stove. Mix all ingredients together. Knead until smooth and shape into a ball. Pinch off a walnut size piece of dough and roll into a 6-inch rope about ½-inch thick. Press ends together to form a circle. Drop circles into boiling water until they rise to the top. Do this a few at a time. Remove from water and dry on the clean towel. Place circles on greased baking dish. Bake 40–50 minutes until golden brown.

I spent many hours standing at the counter that faced the stove in my mother's kitchen and watched her cook. As she made the taralles, she spoke the instructions, yet they were never in precise amounts. Teaspoons, tablespoons, cups – these measurements were useless details to my mother. Cooking was so natural to her, and it seemed she was always in a hurry so it looked as if she was just putting things together without thinking. Looking back, that wasn't the case. She was a busy woman, with a lot of things to do! Taralles were not something she made often, but her acute intuitive cooking sense, and her strong independence, caused her to cook without too much instruction or preciseness. Her dishes always turned out well. In fact, I cannot remember my mother ever preparing a bad meal. Her meals were always put together simply, fast and well. Fortunately, Lorrie somehow managed to get a complete recipe from her which takes the guess-work out of it.

TO SERVE:

Taralles are wonderful served with a glass of wine and a side of fennel and olives.

This simple and delicious salad tastes best if it's made when tomatoes and basil are in season, that is, fresh and plentiful. Choose red, juicy tomatoes, and fresh, tender basil leaves. Add a good quality fresh mozzarella cheese, and you have a delicious appetizer or salad.

Mozzarella and Tomatoes – *Insalata Caprese*

Serves: 4–6

INGREDIENTS:

1 pound fresh mozzarella cheese, sliced ¼ inch

2–3 large, fresh tomatoes

1 cup fresh basil leaves

¼ cup olive oil

2–3 tablespoons aged balsamic vinegar (optional)

Coarse salt and ground pepper to taste

METHOD:

Slice the cheese and tomatoes. Salt the tomatoes, and top with cheese slices and fresh basil on each slice. Add salt and pepper. Olive oil may darken basil leaves, so drizzle with olive oil just before serving. May also be layered on top of rounds or slices of Italian bread.

TO SERVE:

Looks best served on a round serving plate, overlapping the slices. Add fresh basil leaves to the center of plate as a garnish.

A Word About Olive Oil

Olive oil is another one of those ingredients in Italian cooking, much like tomatoes, that is highly revered in the Italian-American kitchen. My mother used olive oil for everything she cooked. She purchased it in a gallon metal can and kept it in a cabinet not far from the stove. I do not recall the brand, but I remember that the can was highly decorated metal with gold and black lettering. No matter what the state of the family budget was, my mother purchased the best olive oil she could afford because she knew how important it was in the meals she prepared. She advised me to do the same.

Today, there is a lot more information available about quality and types of olive oil, including extra-virgin olive oil. My Grandma Castellano believed in the miracle properties of olive oil. Not only did she use it for cooking, she used it on her skin and as a hair treatment. Many warm spring and summer days, she would call my cousin Angela and me outside to sit on folding chairs in the sun while she massaged olive oil into our faces and scalps. When we protested that the olive oil was running into our eyes, she waved away our complaints saying, "One day you'll be glad I did this because it will make your skin and hair beautiful."

Just about every recipe listed calls for olive oil even though a specific type or brand is not included. My mother knew what she was talking about when she said to buy the best olive oil you could afford, and make sure it's the freshest available. Using high quality olive oil will make all the difference in the flavor, appearance and healthful benefits of these recipes.

Lorrie Adds: Every bridal shower I went to as a young girl, and there were many having so many cousins, neighbors and family friends, the one consistent gift was a gallon can of olive oil. That can of olive oil was a rite of passage, an invitation from the adult women in the family to join their group. It was a symbolic key to the door between childhood and adulthood. Your can of olive oil, your very own, not your mother's, secured your place in the adult world of the women in the family. Today, there are other symbols in our family for entering the adult world, such as college degrees, first jobs, or promotions. Yet even today that is the first gift I give to any bride or at any housewarming. The symbolism has changed but the need for a good olive oil has not.

Chapter 5

❧❧❧❧❧

Tomato Sauce ("Gravy") with Meat

Salsa di Pomodoro con Carne

Tomato Sauce ("Gravy") with Meat

Serves: 20

INGREDIENTS:

3½ pounds spare ribs

2 pounds braciole (flank steak or top round, cut thin)

½ pound chopped pork, ½ pound chopped beef, and ½ pound chopped veal

2 lamb shanks, total weight 1½ pounds

4 jars tomatoes or 4 cans San Marzano peeled tomatoes

2 large cans tomato paste

METHOD:

Put tomatoes in a large pot and, using clean hands, break up the whole tomatoes into small pieces. Simmer over a medium flame. Mix meatballs *(see following recipe).* Sauté them to a light brown and set aside in covered dish.

Sauté other meats in a fry pan. Drain off excess fat – anything over ½ cup. If meat is pork, such as sausage or ribs, add immediately to tomatoes and simmer. When tomatoes and pork meat have simmered for 1 hour, add the remainder of the meat to the tomato pot, except the meatballs.

In the same pan used to sauté the meat, add the tomato paste. Fill tomato paste cans with water and add to the paste, blending until the mixture is smooth. Simmer for 20 minutes, slowly, stir often and keep covered when not stirring. Add paste to tomato pot and mix well. If sauce is very thick, thin with a small amount of water. Simmer another 10 minutes. All this time tomato pot is covered. Add meatballs, basil leaves, salt and pepper to taste. Let simmer 20 minutes. Gently stir sauce. Turn off heat. Remove cover slightly.

The longer the sauce sets, the better it tastes. For best results, make this in the morning and serve in the evening. That gives the flavors time to mix well and makes a thick, deep red tomato sauce. Heat the sauce over low heat for about 30 minutes prior to serving.

To cook pasta: Put water onto boil. Add salt. When water is at a rolling boil, add macaroni (pasta) and cook al dente. Just before pasta is ready, remove meat and place on a warm platter. Drain pasta and mix 2 large spoonfuls of sauce to coat the pasta.

TO SERVE:

Place pasta in individual rimmed bowls, top with tomato sauce. Place meat platter on the table to be served family style. Serve with plenty of grated Parmigiano-Reggiano cheese.

For more instructions about cooking pasta, see chapter 6.

A Word About Tomatoes

My mother used homemade canned tomatoes when she made sauce. In later years when she stopped canning, she purchased canned San Marzano tomatoes. San Marzano tomatoes are grown in the Campania region of Italy, which is where her parents were from, and are well known as the great sauce tomatoes.

> *My mother would turn over in her grave if she heard me calling this recipe "Tomato Sauce." She, like so many other Italian-Americans, referred to the luscious red tomato and meat sauce as "gravy." The term "gravy" is still used by our family today.*
>
> *This recipe was dictated to me by my mother as she made it in her kitchen on Bellaire Boulevard in Houston, Texas. I stood at the counter, as I usually did, and watched her and wrote down what she said as she cooked. It is a recipe for six people for four dinners!*
>
> *Many times my mother would get up early on a Sunday morning and make gravy before going to Mass. It was such a comfort to wake up to the smell of her sauce and know that after going to church on Sunday, which I hated doing, that the reward would be to have a nice big plate of meatballs and some type of macaroni (hopefully, rigatoni, my favorite, but any would do!). Sometimes my mother made gravy during the week in the morning so it could set on the stove all day, "with the lid slightly ajar," she reminded me, so all the flavors could blend together.*
>
> *Growing up, "Macaroni night," as it was called, was Tuesdays, Thursdays, and Sundays. Pretty much all Italian-Americans observed this ritual. Rarely would she deviate from this schedule, but if she did we would all be very displeased and grumble about it. Sometimes she varied this recipe, using "what you have," as she put it, but no matter the ingredients, my mother's tomato sauce was always delicious. She used to say that her mother, my Grandma Camille Cibella, taught her, "If you use good ingredients, you get a good meal," and she was right.*
>
> *My mother said this recipe made enough tomato sauce for three meals. But how many people was she talking about feeding? Often family and friends would join us and there was always enough for at least a dozen people. This recipe serves at least 20 people, so feel free to cut it in half, or even in quarters.*

Mom's Meatballs – *Polpette alla Napoletana*

This recipe is a continuation of my mother's tomato sauce instruction.

Serves: 12

INGREDIENTS:

½ pound chopped pork, ½ pound chopped beef, ½ pound chopped veal

3 eggs, beaten with a little milk

4 full tablespoons Italian-style bread crumbs

3 full tablespoons grated cheese

(Note: in my mother's recipes, it is understood that grated cheese was either Parmigiano-Reggiano or Pecorino. She did not differentiate between the two when giving a recipe. It may have been, once again, according to "what you have" on hand.)

¼ cup fresh parsley, chopped, to taste

¼ cup fresh basil, chopped, to taste, or 2 teaspoons dried

4 cloves garlic, chopped

Salt and pepper to taste

Olive oil

METHOD:

Beat eggs with a little milk. Add the remaining ingredients to the egg mixture and mix well. With wet hands, shape meat into balls, 1½–2 inches round. Sauté in olive oil until light brown. Remove and set aside until sauce is ready for meatballs. *(See previous recipe.)*

The smell of meatballs sautéing ranks up there with the top aromas of our Italian-American family kitchen. Smelling olive oil and meat simmering, along with hearing the occasional pops of the olive oil flying because my mother cooked pretty much everything on "high," reminds me of childhood. "Your mother doesn't know low," my father used to say.

My mother made good meatballs – the way her mother taught her – though my father said that no one could make meatballs like his mother, Grandma "Fanny" Castellano. Later on in his retirement years, my father took over making meatballs and tomato sauce, and he did a good job of it too, though he admits he was never quite able to duplicate his mother's meatballs. On some things, Fanny could not be outdone!

VARIATION:

My Grandma Castellano's meatballs surpassed any I've ever eaten. She made large meatballs that were soft inside and held together very well without the outside being crispy or hard. She always used Italian bread, along with Italian bread crumbs in her meatballs. She would cut a large piece of bread off the loaf, preferably the heel, tear it apart with her fingers, and place it in a small bowl of milk. Once the bread softened, she squeezed out most of the milk and added the bread to the meatball mixture. I watched her sauté meatballs for most of my childhood. She used a medium heat and turned the meatballs frequently. She never left the stove while her meatballs were cooking. I vary from my mother's recipe and use Italian bread in my meatballs and make them large, just as my grandmother did.

Braciole – Stuffed Rolled Steak

Serves: 8 slices

INGREDIENTS:

Flank steak or top round, approximately 1½ pounds cut thin

2 cloves garlic, minced

⅔ cup Pecorino or Romano cheese, grated

4 tablespoons fresh Italian parsley leaves, chopped

1 teaspoon basil, dried

Salt and ground pepper

Butcher's twine

METHOD:

Lay flank steak flat. Spread garlic on the meat. Sprinkle salt, pepper, cheese, parsley and basil evenly over the steak. Starting at the short end, roll up the steak like a jelly roll. Using butcher's twine, tie the steak roll to secure. Sauté in medium-hot olive oil until steak is lightly browned, turning frequently. Add to tomato sauce and let simmer with the other meats until sauce is finished cooking. Remove from sauce and let it cool.

TO SERVE:

Slice and serve as described.

> *My mother usually added this tasty meat to her tomato sauce. It's a simple recipe and takes just a few minutes to prepare for cooking. When it is finally cooked, the meat is very tender and can be cut with a fork. This may make it difficult to serve, but my mother had the answer to that. She taught me to remove the braciole from the tomato pot first, allowing it to cool a bit. When cool, snip the twine with kitchen scissors and slice the meat into small pieces, which look like pinwheels, and drizzle a small amount of hot tomato sauce over each slice. The platter was then filled in the middle with meat balls, sausage, ribs or whatever other meats she prepared and placed in the center of the table with a large serving fork. This makes for a mighty and appetizing presentation.*

Tomato Sauce with Sausage – *Salsa di Pomodoro con Salsiccia*

Tomato sauce using only sausage is a quick, easy way to make a sauce that can be served over pasta or polenta.

Serves: 4

INGREDIENTS:

1 pound sweet or hot Italian sausage

2 large cans of Italian tomatoes

2 cloves garlic, minced

1 small onion, finely chopped

4 tablespoons fresh basil, or 1 teaspoon dried

1 pinch of oregano, dried

Salt and pepper

2 tablespoons olive oil

METHOD:

Sauté onions in olive oil over medium heat, then add garlic and continue to sauté. In a separate frying pan, add sausage and brown slightly on all sides. Puncture sausage with large fork to allow fat to escape. Drain off fat. Combine all ingredients and simmer for about 1 hour.

TO SERVE:

Serve on pasta or polenta with grated cheese sprinkled on top.

Marinara sauce was something my mother could whip up in a matter of minutes. If she had been out all day (rarely when we were little) or if she was involved in a big project, like sewing or canning, this is the meal she'd make. Like my mother, marinara sauce has turned out to be one of my quick "go to" recipes today when I need a pasta fix and don't have time to make a big pot of tomato sauce with meat.

Mom's Meatless Tomato Sauce – Marinara Sauce

Serves: 4

INGREDIENTS:

2 large yellow onions, peeled and diced

4 tablespoons olive oil

6 cloves garlic, minced

2 large cans whole, peeled tomatoes

2 tablespoons basil and oregano, dried

¼ teaspoon red pepper flakes or to taste

Salt and pepper, to taste

METHOD:

In large pot, heat olive oil. Sauté onions until they are soft. Add garlic, dried herbs and pepper flakes and cook for about 5 minutes. Place tomatoes in a bowl and crush with hands to break up tomatoes. Add crushed tomatoes to pot. Salt and pepper to taste. Simmer for about 30 minutes or longer if you have time.

TO SERVE:

Serve over spaghetti or favorite pasta.

Mom's Quick Fresh Tomato Sauce – *Pasta con Pomodoro*

This is from a handwritten collection of recipes from my mother. When fresh tomatoes were plentiful, especially during canning time, this is another version of a quick marinara sauce.

Serves: 4

INGREDIENTS:

10–12 fresh plum tomatoes (approximately 2–2½ pounds)

4 ounces olive oil, plus 2–3 additional tablespoons

½ medium onion, chopped

3 cloves garlic, chopped

2 tablespoons tomato paste

Handful fresh basil, chopped, or 1 teaspoon dried basil

Pinch of crushed red pepper

Salt and pepper to taste

METHOD:

Prepare tomatoes by scoring the skin with a sharp knife, making an X. Be careful not to score too deeply. Place scored tomatoes into a pot of boiling water for approximately 1 minute. Remove with slotted spoon and place in a bowl of cold water. Peel and remove skin and seed and dice. Heat olive oil in a large saucepan. Add garlic and crushed red pepper. Sauté until garlic is slightly golden. Add onion and sauté another 2–3 minutes or until onions are soft. Add tomato paste and plum tomatoes, mix well, and simmer approximately 5 minutes. Add the basil, saving a little for garnish. Salt and pepper to taste.

TO SERVE:

Moisten cooked pasta with 2 spoonfuls of sauce, mixing well. Serve in rimmed soup bowl, adding sauce on the pasta and sprinkling some fresh basil on top. Place grated cheese on the table.

Joe's Italian Sausage – Salsiccia Italiano

Occasionally my mother would make homemade Italian sausage, using a large, bulky grinder. I still marvel at how she did all the things she did, including making sausage, when she could easily buy it at the butcher shop. My mother wrote down two Italian sausage recipes, one of which was stuffed in the box that contained the sausage grinder. She gave the grinder to my brother, Joe, and he and his family carry on the sausage-making tradition today using that same grinder. Joe has raised my mother's recipe to new heights and perfected it to just the right taste. When I asked him for the recipe, this is the email he sent:

"Attached you will find Mom's recipe that was stuffed in the box with the grinder. Her recipe has ½ cup of salt way too much. This is the way we make it…"

SWEET SAUSAGE

Serves: makes about 17 pounds of sausage

INGREDIENTS:

Sausage grinder

1 large box of commercial clear plastic wrap

20 pounds pork butt, cut lean and ground twice by the butcher. It should look like chili meat. This breaks down any fatty strings.

A little less than ¼ cup of salt

9 teaspoons of black pepper

1¼ cups fennel seeds, crushed with a rolling pin

1½ bunches Italian parsley, chopped

1 hank of sheep intestines

1 cup warm water

HOT SAUSAGE

Same as above except add ½ cup red pepper flakes.

(Jay and I make what we call Super Hot by taking 3 pounds sweet meat and adding ½ cup of pepper flakes, it's good when cooked with sausage and peppers and/or potatoes, AWESOME!)

Elizabeth and I can make 17 pounds of sausage, wrapped in 1-pound wheels and clean up in about 2½ hours. Wrap each wheel about 6 times in clear plastic wrap. This will protect it from the freezer for up to 8 months. If you want I'll send you Mom's machine to make a batch, just send it back or I'll send my boys to visit. Enjoy and let me know how it goes.

Joe adds the following instructions regarding mixing and stuffing the sausage:

From a full service butcher, purchase a hank of sheep intestines packed in salt. Keep the packaging, including the salt and the liquid. You'll need this to repack the extras/leftover skins. Place in the refrigerator or freezer for future use. These skins will last at least a year. Separate the strings from the hank and soak in fresh water and rinse them to get the salt out. It's the same process as baccala. Place the skins in a bowl with water and place to the side for now; you will need the extra water during the stuffing process.

After the meat is mixed make a small patty and fry it up to taste the flavor of the meat. Here comes the tricky part. The meat and spices have not had enough time to blend. When you taste the meat, if the salt or spice is not overpowering you'll be good.

Experience has taught me that if you follow the recipe you'll make excellent sausage. I use less salt because Mom and Dad gave me the gift of high blood pressure and less salt makes me feel less like I'm cheating on my doctor.

Before the stuffing begins, add 1 cup warm water to the meat and mix in well to make the stuffing process easier. Make large meatball-size balls of meat before you start stuffing the sausage. Take the skins from the bowl of water and slide them over the funnel on the stuffing machine dripping water on the casing during the process. It's important to keep the skins wet during the entire process. Tie a knot in the end of the casing to begin the wheel. Keep the skin on the funnel wet.

Now you're ready to begin. If you have a machine like the one my mother gave to me you will need two people. One person to feed the meat into the stuffer and crank and the other person to control how much meat goes into the casing. This is done by holding the funnel with one hand placing slight pressure on the skin to make sure it fills to 1-inch-thick sausage link. If in the beginning you have some air close to the knot of the skin, just puncture a small hole close to the knot and massage the air out. As the casing is stuffed, allow the sausage to roll into large wheels on the cooking surface dripping water on it along the way until the casing has about 6 inches left on the funnel. Slide the casing off the funnel and tie into a knot.

Repeat the process as needed until all the meat is used. When completely finished stuffing all the meat, you can decide if you want to make sausage links. Determine how long you want the link. Pinch the sausage and give it a twist. No need to tie the ends after they are cut because the meat has had time to set and you'll be okay.

Start the wrapping process with the smaller wheels. The major cause of freezer burn is the lack of protection around the meat. We use a commercial size box of clear plastic kitchen wrap and wrap the wheels at least six times each. This protects the meat and will last six to eight months in the freezer with no burn. Make sure the first layer or two does not have any excess air in the wrapper. If they do, puncture the wrap with the tip of a knife and push the air out. Continue with another six or eight layers of wrap. Before you place the last layer of wrap write a note indicating the type of sausage (sweet, hot, or super hot) and the date. This way you know what you're about to cook prior to cooking.

It's okay to get experimental with the sausage—add garlic or pine nuts and cheese. Enjoy!

Chapter 6

Pasta

A Word About Pasta

Italians like to eat pasta that is cooked "al dente," literally meaning "to the tooth," or just slightly firm when bitten.

INGREDIENTS:

Pasta

Large pot of boiling water — 4 quarts of water for every 4 ounces of pasta

1–2 tablespoons of coarse salt per pound of pasta

METHOD:

Begin with a large, tall pot to give the pasta plenty of room to cook in salted, boiling water. When water is boiling, add pasta. Stir frequently. Cooking times will vary. For dried pasta, check the directions on the package. Freshly made or store-bought fresh pasta cooks quickly, so check often. To test for doneness, remove a piece of pasta and break it apart to check for a tiny, white dot in the center. That indicates that it is al dente. You can also taste it for firmness. The pasta should be chewy and slightly firm.

When done, remove immediately from heat and drain in a colander. Return to pot and add a cup of whatever sauce you're using and mix thoroughly through the pasta. This will prevent it from sticking. My mother never added olive oil to her cooked pasta and she never rinsed it. Rinsing will not only cool the pasta, but will remove the starch which is necessary for the sauce to stick to the pasta.

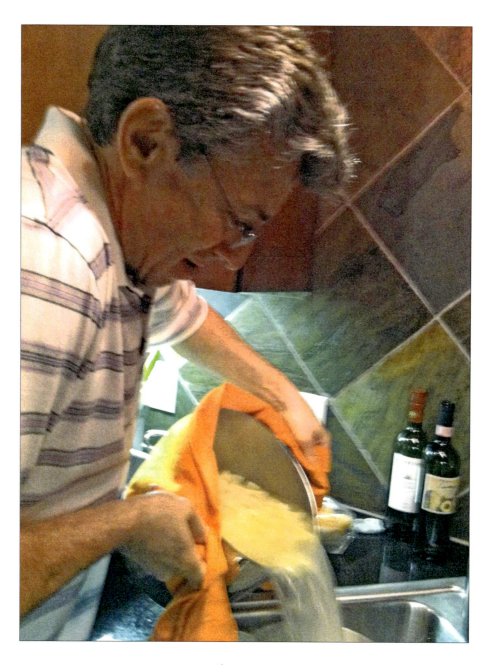

Joe draining pasta

Linguini and Clams – *Linguini e vongole*

Serves: 4

INGREDIENTS:

1 pound linguini, cooked al dente

1 bag Little Neck Clams (or 10–12 per person). If fresh isn't available, canned clams work very well – 2 large cans clams, chopped

1 bottle clam juice

⅓ cup olive oil

3 large cloves garlic, minced

Dried red pepper flakes, to taste

½ cup fresh flat leaf Italian parsley, chopped

METHOD:

If using fresh clams, rinse clams in cold water, making sure each clam is closed. If they are open, discard – do not use an open, fresh clam!

Heat olive oil. Sauté garlic lightly. If using canned clams, add clams, reserving the liquid. Add salt, pepper, red pepper flakes to taste, stir, and then add reserved clam liquid and bottle of clam juice. Cover and simmer about 2 minutes. If using fresh clams, follow the same directions except you'll know the clams are cooked when they open.

TO SERVE:

Serve over linguini cooked al dente. Place individual servings of linguini in rimmed bowls, add clams and clam sauce, sprinkle liberally with fresh parsley. Serve right away.

VARIATION:

After one of my trips to Italy, I started sprinkling a little bit of breadcrumbs on the cooked linguini, mixing it well, before adding the clam sauce. I learned this after having a fantastic bowl of linguini and clams in Venice where the waiter shared with me what made the sauce seem a little creamy. I never made it that way for my father. I don't think he would have approved!

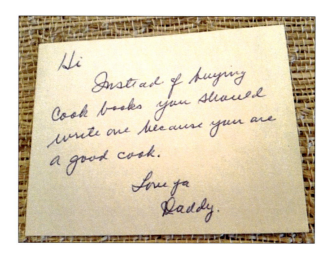

This, along with spaghetti aglio e olio, was one of my father's favorite dishes. Growing up, my mother served this meal often, especially on Friday nights, in the days when meat wasn't eaten on Fridays in the Catholic tradition. My mother would make a white or red sauce, mainly a white sauce, since that was my father's favorite. Making this dish reminds me of some very happy times in Houston, Texas, when my mother and father would come to my house on Linden Street for dinner and I would serve this dish. My father ate linguini with gusto and joy, and he always told me I made the best linguini and clams! I guess that was a compliment to my mother as well, because I learned it from her. My father always said that if you want to know if an Italian restaurant is a good one (that is, what he considered good – which was the way his mother and his wife cooked), then order linguini and clams and judge for yourself.

Spaghetti with Olive Oil – *Spaghetti Aglio e olio*

Serves: 4

INGREDIENTS:

1 pound of spaghetti, cooked al dente

¼ cup olive oil

10 cloves garlic, thinly sliced

Salt and pepper to taste

1 teaspoon dried red pepper flakes

¼ cup fresh parsley, chopped

Parmigiano-Reggiano, grated for serving

METHOD:

Sauté garlic in olive oil until lightly brown (about 2 minutes). Add pepper flakes and parsley and remove from heat. Combine cooked spaghetti and olive oil mixture, adding about ⅓ cup pasta water to help coat spaghetti.

TO SERVE:

This is one dish that must be served immediately. Plate it right away. My mother always said it dries out very quickly. Place grated cheese on the table to sprinkle on top of pasta.

My mother and father shared stories about when they were younger and would go out with their friends to clubs to dance and have a few drinks. This was the dish they came home to in the wee hours. Since all the restaurants were closed by the time they left the clubs, they would invite hungry friends over, and my mother would whip up this dish.

Mom's Cavatelli

Serves: 4

INGREDIENTS:

2½ cups all purpose flour

⅛ teaspoon salt

1 large egg

1 large egg yolk

½ cup water

METHOD:

Place the flour on a wooden board or clean kitchen counter and make a well in it. Crack the egg and egg yolk in a small bowl and beat. Add water to the eggs and beat again. Add eggs to the well in the flour. Add salt. Then use a fork and work in the majority of the flour from the edges a little at a time until the egg mixture becomes one sticky ball. Coat your hands with flour and gently knead the remaining flour into an elastic ball of dough. Wrap dough in plastic wrap and refrigerate for 1 hour.

Clamp the machine onto the edge of a counter or table. Cut the ball of dough into 3 pieces and cover with a clean, damp kitchen towel. Take each piece of dough, one at a time, and roll into long "ropes" of dough, approximately ½-inch thick and feed it through the machine.

If forming the cavatelli by hand, cut the ½-inch thick ropes into ½-inch pieces. Dust lightly with flour. Take each ½-inch piece and using your middle and ring fingers, roll the dough downward and towards you to form the shape.

Place the cavatelli pieces on a floured surface for 1 hour or longer until ready to cook.

TO SERVE:

Cook cavatelli al dente, about 4 minutes, or until the first few float to the top of the water. Drain and coat with about 1 cup sauce and mix well. Serve in rimmed bowl with grated cheese.

This recipe says it is for four people, but I don't ever remember my mother making so few! She may have modified the recipe for me when I asked her for it. My mother was a master at making homemade pasta. She made it all her life, learning it at home with her own mother. It amazes me now that with all her family responsibilities, she still had time to make "homemade macaroni." She made a lot of different kinds of homemade pasta, including ravioli, fettuccini, manicotti and spaghetti. Cavatelli was another of my dad's favorites, along with ravioli. I think this recipe predates the manual "cavatelli maker," which is a simple hand cranked device that attaches to a table. This little device was a great time saver, and she used it whenever she could. My job was to help form the long "ropes" from which the cavatelli shape would be cut. The "rope" had to be just the right circumference, and if it wasn't, I had to start over.

When I got a little older, my mother taught me how to actually roll the cavatelli into shape, and I was so proud of myself for being able to maneuver my middle and ring finger on the one-inch section of dough to get the shape right. When I got it right, I knew she was pleased, because she would give me a little nod of approval.

Homemade macaroni has to be dried for a few hours and, as Lorrie described earlier, my mother would spread clean, white sheets out on anything she could find – tables, counter tops, even beds, to dry the macaroni. To this day, I have never made cavatelli by myself. It used to be with my mother. Today, my son, Jeremy Jones, carries on the tradition, using the same cavatelli maker that was my mother's. My job is still to help make the ropes, and, of course, turn the crank.

Nothing to me says Italian more than a bowl of homemade cavatelli.

    This was and still is the ultimate child's comfort food in our family. It was the quick default dish my mother and Grandma Castellano used for anything that might ail us. No matter the reason, such as "I'm hungry," "My stomach hurts," "I feel sad," "I'm worried," "I don't know what I want to eat," pastina with the egg fits the bill. Why it is called with "the" egg, I do not know. My cousin Angela Castellano Cosgrove, who was raised by our Grandma Castellano and was frequently served this dish, always called it "a nice bowl of pastina with the egg." That is how revered it was and is to her. As a toddler and young boy, my son Jeremy, loved eating pastina. I can still see him sitting in his high chair clapping his hands in anticipation while the pastina cooked on the stove. I would venture to guess that there is not an Italian-American in the U.S. that was not raised on this dish!

    As usual, it is simple, quick and delicious. Unlike a lot of the recipes my mother and grandmother made, this one is made in small amounts, usually 1 or 2 servings, depending on the circumstances. Even today, I make a bowl for myself when I am feeling the need for a little fast comfort food.

Pastina with 'the' Egg

Serves: 1

INGREDIENTS:

3–4 tablespoons of pastina

1 egg beaten with a dash of milk

1 tablespoon butter

Salt to taste

METHOD:

Boil water in a small sauce pan. Add pastina and cook for 5 or 6 minutes, until soft. Drain, leaving a little of the pastina water in the pan. Returning the pastina and the little bit of water to the stove over heat, add the beaten egg, stirring until it is cooked. Add salt to taste.

TO SERVE:

Place in a small bowl, add a dollop of butter and serve hot.

LORRIE ADDS:

Pastina is the only pasta that should never be cooked al dente. It should be well cooked so it's soft and goes down easy. Whenever my daughter, Torry, had one of those bad, awful, hard, no-good days when she was growing up, I'd say, 'Let's have some pastina.' It always worked. It's soothing to the soul. It makes all your problems go away. It's the magic pill for everything that ails you. When my grandchildren were born, I made them pastina whenever we were together. Now the first thing they say when they enter my door is 'Can I have some pastina, Noni?' I make it with or without "the" egg. Without the egg, you just cook the pastina, add some butter and salt and there it is: the perfect comfort food.

Peas and Pasta – *Piselli e Pasta*

Serves: 4

INGREDIENTS:

2 cans petite green peas

1 pound small pasta, such as ditalini

1 onion, finely chopped

½ teaspoon oregano, dried

Olive oil

Salt and pepper

Parmesan cheese

METHOD:

Cook the pasta in boiling salted water for 10 minutes. While pasta is cooking, sauté the chopped onion in olive oil. When the onions are soft and translucent, add the peas, dried oregano and salt and pepper. Simmer for a few minutes to allow the flavors to blend. Drain the pasta, return to the pan and add the peas. Stir and heat through.

TO SERVE:

Serve immediately, steaming hot and sprinkled with some Parmesan cheese.

My Grandma Castellano prepared this dish often. She passed her love of it onto my father, so my mother prepared it often for him. On cold winter days, this was a dish Grandma prepared at lunchtime for my cousin Angela and me. She always served it with Italian bread and butter.

Fusilli, Ziti or Cavatelli with Broccoli or Cauliflower – *Fusilli, Ziti o Cavatelli con Broccoli o Cavolfiore*

Serves: 4–6

INGREDIENTS:

1 pound of fusilli, ziti, cavatelli or any other sturdy pasta of that size

1 head of fresh cauliflower, quartered and core removed and/or 1 bunch fresh broccoli, trimmed of tough ends

4 large cloves garlic, chopped

2 medium yellow onions, sliced

1 teaspoon oregano, dried

1 cup grated Parmigiano-Reggiano cheese

Olive oil

Generous pinch of hot pepper flakes

Salt and pepper to taste

1 cup pasta water just in case it is dry

METHOD:

Slice broccoli stems crosswise into ¼-inch slices. Slice florets lengthwise. Cut cauliflower into similar size pieces as broccoli. In a large sauté pan, heat up enough olive oil to cover the bottom of the pan and add the broccoli and/or cauliflower. Add salt and cook broccoli and/or cauliflower until tender and a little browned in spots. Remove and set aside. In the same pan, sauté onions and when they begin to soften, add garlic, hot pepper flakes and a pinch of salt. Sauté 1–2 minutes until garlic softens but is not brown. Set aside. When pasta is cooked and drained, add all other ingredients and oregano and mix well. Add pasta water if dry. Taste to make sure seasonings are correct.

TO SERVE:

Serve immediately in rimmed soup bowl and topped with grated Parmesan cheese.

Fusilli with broccoli

This healthy dish can be made with ziti or any pasta of that size or with either homemade or store-bought cavatelli. My mother whipped this dish up in a hurry, usually using ziti or mostacelli, and it always tasted delicious. If she didn't have fresh broccoli or cauliflower, she'd use frozen. Either way it turned out fine. It's a hearty dish and it doesn't take much to feel filled up.

Lorrie's *Pasta e Fagioli*

Serves: 4

INGREDIENTS:

3 tablespoons olive oil

1 clove garlic, chopped

2 cans cannellini beans

1 pound pasta, dilatini, or other small pasta

¼ teaspoon oregano, dried

Small handful chopped fresh basil or 1 teaspoon dried basil

Salt and pepper

METHOD:

Sauté garlic in olive oil until soft but not browned. Add cannellini beans, oregano and basil. Let simmer to heat beans and mix flavors. While simmering, mash about half the beans so the rest of the beans are swimming in a creamy looking sauce. Cook pasta in salted boiling water until al dente. Combine the pasta and beans. Salt and pepper to taste. Heat through and serve.

VARIATION:

Add a jar of your canned tomatoes or your favorite brand of whole or crushed tomatoes to the beans. This is when you'll be glad you canned your own tomatoes. If adding tomatoes, sauté some red pepper flakes in with the garlic. Be careful, a little goes a long way. When my son, Larry, comes to dinner, I add more than usual because he loves this dish very spicy.

TO SERVE:

Serve with a sprinkle of Parmesan cheese and a leafy green salad.

Pasta 'Fazool' – *Pasta e Fagioli*

Serves: 4

INGREDIENTS:

1 cup small pasta, such as tubettini or ditalini

2 cans cooked small white cannellini beans, drained, and reserve liquid

4 tablespoons olive oil, plus additional for drizzling

1 small onion, finely chopped

2 medium cloves garlic, minced

10 fresh sage leaves, finely chopped

3 tablespoons tomato paste

Parmigiano-Reggiano cheese, grated

Salt and pepper to taste

METHOD:

Cook pasta until partially cooked, usually about 5 minutes. Drain and set aside. Heat olive oil in large sauce pan over medium heat. Sauté onions until soft. Add garlic and sage and cook for about 1 minute. Season with salt and pepper and stir in tomato paste, mixing well. Thin mixture with some of the bean liquid. Take ¼ cup cooked beans and mash with a fork and add this and the beans to the mixture. Simmer for 10 minutes. Add pasta and simmer about 5 minutes, making sure the pasta is al dente.

TO SERVE:

Place in a rimmed bowl. Sprinkle grated cheese and drizzle a little olive oil on top. Serve immediately.

> *True to the southern Italian dialect, this dish was called Pasta Fazool when I was growing up and was found on most every Italian-American table. This recipe was created based on the most delicious Pasta e Fagioli I ever tasted when I was Venice in 2000. While wandering the narrow paths along the many canals there, we came upon a tiny bar called VinoVino. There were eight small tables in the place, rows and rows of wine bottles, and a chalkboard with the day's specials. That day it was pasta e fagioli. VinoVino's rendition was similar to my mother's, but with less pasta and more beans and sage. I enjoyed this dish so much I went back that night and had it again.*

Chickpeas and Pasta – *Ceci e Pasta*

Pasta "Fazool" and Ceci and Pasta are two dishes that you can make any time of day or night because the ingredients can be stored in your pantry and be ready for use in a moment's notice: canned cannellini beans, garbanzo beans, any kind of pasta, and home-canned tomatoes or store-bought tomatoes.

Serves: 4

INGREDIENTS:

½ onion, chopped

3 tablespoons olive oil

1 can garbanzo beans

1 pound small pasta, elbows, ditalini, small shells or other bite-size pasta

¼ teaspoon dried oregano or 1 teaspoon fresh oregano

Small handful of fresh basil, chopped, or 1 teaspoon dried basil

Salt and pepper

METHOD:

Sauté onion in olive oil until soft and translucent. Add can of garbanzo beans, oregano and basil. Cook pasta in salted boiling water, al dente. Drain and return to the pan. Add the beans to the pasta and heat through. Add salt and pepper to taste.

TO SERVE:

Serve piping hot and sprinkled with Parmesan cheese. A green salad completes this meal.

Ladies of the Night Pasta – *Pasta alla Puttanesca*

This is one of those fast pastas that the Ladies of the Night made after a hard day's work. It has the kind of ingredients you can keep in your pantry and be ready to make at a moment's notice. It has the advantage of looking like you've been cooking all day!

Serves: 4

INGREDIENTS:

1 pound spaghetti, pappardelle, penne or rigatoni

¼ cup olive oil

1 small onion, chopped

4 cloves garlic finely chopped

⅛ teaspoon red pepper flakes (more if you like your sauce spicy)

8 fillets of anchovy, finely chopped (canned will do nicely)

2 cans tomatoes or 2 jars of your home-canned tomatoes

2 tablespoons capers, rinsed and drained

1 cup pitted, halved calamata olives

Small handful of chopped fresh basil

Handful of chopped Italian parsley

Salt and pepper

METHOD:

Sauté onion, garlic and red pepper flakes in olive oil until the onion and garlic are soft. Add the anchovy fillets. Sauté for a minute. Add the cans of tomatoes, basil and oregano. Simmer for about 30 minutes. Add capers and olives. Let simmer 10 more minutes while you cook the pasta. Drain the pasta well and return to the pot. Add one ladle of the sauce and stir to coat pasta.

TO SERVE:

Fill bowls with pasta, pour sauce over the pasta, sprinkle with chopped parsley. Serve with a crisp, fresh salad.

Ingredients for Pasta Puttanesca

Grandma Castellano's Bows with Pot Cheese – *Farfalle alla Ricotta*

Serves: 4

INGREDIENTS:

1 pound bow ties (farfalle)

1 pound ricotta cheese

½ cup Parmigiano cheese, grated

2 eggs, beaten

½ cup fresh Italian flat-leaf parsley, chopped

Salt and pepper to taste

METHOD:

Combine pot cheese, Parmigiano cheese, beaten eggs and parsley. Mix well. Cook pasta al dente. Moisten the cooked pasta with about 1 cup tomato sauce, then add the pot cheese mixture and mix gently. Put in bowl and cover with additional tomato sauce.

TO SERVE:

Serve this dish immediately in a rimmed bowl and top with tomato sauce. Place grated cheese on table.

As mentioned before, Grandma Fanny Castellano was a fantastic cook. Everything she made, from the simplest lunches to her fabulous meatballs, was delicious. When I was a little girl, sometimes we'd go to her house on Mt. Prospect Avenue on Sundays and have this dish. As Lorrie described, our grandmother had a long wooden dining room table and it would be set when we arrived with her pretty china, silver and crystal. The kitchen was separated from the dining room by a white wooden swinging door, and I can still see her coming through that door with a large platter of meatballs, sausage and other meats, which she set in the middle of the table. Then came the individual bowls filled with bows with pot cheese (ricotta). This deliciously creamy dish would be steaming hot and smelling so good, it was hard to wait for everyone to be served so we could say "Grace."

Later on, when she lived with my Uncle Nick on Highland Avenue in Newark and took care of him and my cousin Angela, she would buy pot cheese on Sunday morning after Mass. She made her tomato sauce early that morning before Mass, so it set all morning and part of the afternoon, and the flavors blended well to produce a thick, rich red sauce. Occasionally on Saturday night I would spend the night at their house. Uncle Nick, Grandma, Angela and I would go to Sacred Heart Cathedral in Newark, New Jersey, for Sunday Mass. After Mass, Uncle Nick would stop at Ferrara's Bakery on Bloomfield Avenue so Grandma could pick up fresh pot cheese. It was always crowded at Ferrara's after church because every other Italian-American woman in the neighborhood was doing the same thing my Grandma was doing – picking up her pot cheese for Sunday dinner. Uncle Nick would have to double park while Grandma would go in to make her purchase. Sometimes she would let Angela and me go in with her. I loved going in there because it smelled so good. Fresh baked bread, huge varieties of Italian pastries and cookies were beautifully displayed in this small store. Ricotta cheese was made right there too. Back then, the cheese was packed in a tall, thin, silver-colored metal pot and covered with a square of white waxed paper and secured around with white string. That is how it got its name "pot cheese."

Mom's Lasagna – *Lasagna di Carnevale*

Serves: 6 generous portions or 8 smaller ones

INGREDIENTS:

1 pound lasagna sheets

1 large ball of mozzarella cheese, grated, or 1 pound fresh mozzarella, sliced

½ pound Parmesan cheese grated

2 pounds ricotta cheese

2 eggs, beaten

Prepare tomato sauce and meatballs in Chapter 5

Handful of chopped parsley

Salt and pepper

METHOD:

Cook lasagna sheets according to directions on the box. Drain and cool by a spray of cold water and lay out individually on clean kitchen towels. Dry by patting each lasagna sheet so that all water is absorbed. This is an important step so don't be tempted to skip it. The lasagna will be watery otherwise. Prepare tomato sauce and meatballs as described in Chapter 5. However, make the meatballs tiny (1 inch in diameter). This can be done ahead of time. Set aside. Mix ricotta cheese with the eggs, a handful of Parmesan cheese, a handful of parsley, salt and pepper. Set aside. Place sliced or grated mozzarella and grated Parmesan cheese on separate plates. Set aside.

Now you are ready to put all the pieces together and make great lasagna. Spread one ladle of sauce on the bottom of a 9-inch by 13-inch oven proof pan. Line bottom of pan with lasagna sheets. With a large spoon scoop up dollops of ricotta cheese mixture and spread it thickly and evenly on the lasagna sheets. Layer with mozzarella. Sprinkle with Parmesan cheese. Ladle out sauce and tiny meatballs and spread meatballs so they are evenly distributed. Layer the top with lasagna sheets and begin the layering process until you reach the top of the pan. You should be able to make three layers.

The last layer ends with the lasagna sheets, tomato sauce and whatever Parmesan cheese and mozzarella you have left.

Place in a preheated oven at 350° for 45 minutes or until you see the sauce bubbling and the cheese melting.

TO SERVE:

Let stand for 10–15 minutes before slicing.

LORRIE ADDS:

This dish freezes well so it can be made ahead of time. If you freeze it, cover it with plastic wrap and then aluminum foil. It will need several hours to defrost before you're ready to cook it. I always serve this as a side dish for Thanksgiving to bring a little Italy into our American holiday.

> *My mother's lasagna was always thick, rich and densely packed. She usually made it for holidays or special occasions, as it was time-consuming to make. My mother used to say that lasagna was the best dish to serve when you were having dinner guests because it could be made in advance, and baked in the oven when guests arrived. That way, you could enjoy your company without being in the kitchen the entire time. I loved when she made lasagna because she always made a lot so there were leftovers, which we could have for lunch. What a treat! Lorrie was able to get the complete recipe. My mother always made a huge pot of tomato sauce, larger than usual, for this dish, with little meatballs for easier layering. She said that lasagna soaked up the sauce.*

Cappellini & Anchovies – *Cappellini e Acciughe*

SEE CHAPTER 11 CHRISTMAS EVE

Mom's Ravioli – *Ravioli alla Napoletana*

Serves 6

INGREDIENTS:

3 cups flour

1 teaspoon salt

2 tablespoons olive oil

1 cup warm water

4 eggs

2 pounds ricotta cheese

Large handful finely chopped Italian parsley

Large handful grated Parmesan cheese

Salt and pepper to taste

METHOD:

Place the flour on a wooden board in a mound. In the center of the mound make a hole and add 2 eggs, the olive oil, and the salt. Slowly add the water, combining all ingredients. Knead and fold the dough until it's smooth and elastic but not sticky. If it's sticky, add some flour. Coat the dough in olive oil and let it "rest" while you make the ricotta mixture. Place the ricotta in a large bowl. Add 2 eggs, parsley and Parmesan cheese, salt and pepper, and mix.

Using a rolling pin or a pasta-making machine, roll out small pieces of the dough into thin strips 16 inches by 4 inches. Flour the surfaces to insure the dough doesn't stick. Every 4 inches place a tablespoon or two (depending on taste) of the ricotta mixture onto the dough. Over that, place another 16-inch-by-4-inch sheet of rolled-out dough. Cut between the "pillows" and, using the tines of a fork, seal the ravioli on all four sides. Repeat until all the dough has been used.

Ravioli needs to be cooked in a big pot of boiling water so they don't stick to each other. Put your pot on to boil. While waiting for it to boil, prick two holes in the top of each ravioli with a toothpick. Place each ravioli into the boiling water very carefully. Cook for about 4 minutes. The ravioli will float to the top when they are cooked. Use a slotted spoon to retrieve them from the boiling water.

TO SERVE:

Serve in rimmed soup bowls, carefully coating with a light tomato sauce.

Mom making ravioli

As Lorrie mentioned, making ravioli was a family endeavor. This is a bit labor-intensive, yet worth it. My mother loved making ravioli, and she depended on her children to help with the many small steps of the process. Lorrie was able to get this recipe from my mother, complete with measurements. Amazing!

Castelvatrono olives

Chapter 7

SALADS

No Italian meal is complete without some type of salad. Growing up, there was usually a leafy green salad at supper, dressed with a simple Italian dressing. Italian-Americans love greens and serve them cold or hot. Typically, salad is served after the entrée, not with the main dish. My mother's salads were always delicious. She made sure that the salad greens were soaked in cool water, rinsed well and drained. Whatever type of greens she had on hand appeared in the salad. We grew up eating all kinds of leaf lettuce, including frisee, radicchio, dandelions, chicory, romaine, arugula and escarole. Salad dressing was made fresh every night. I was a young adult before I tasted prepared bottled salad dressings. My mother would whip up the dressing quickly, wash her hands thoroughly, then dress the salad, mixing gently with her hands. My brother Joe comes closest to my mother in preparing a delicious salad and dressing, mixed with his hands.

Leafy Green Salad – *Foglia Insalata Verde*

Serves: 8

INGREDIENTS:

6 cups mixed greens (frisee, radicchio, dandelions, chicory, romaine, arugula, escarole or "whatever you have") – washed, drained and torn into small pieces

6 tomatoes, quartered

METHOD:

Combine greens and tomatoes. Dress with salad dressing below.

TO SERVE:

If prepared in advance, cover with plastic wrap and refrigerate. Place in large bowl and dress salad right before serving.

Italian Salad Dressing – *Condimenti per Insalata*

Serves: 8

INGREDIENTS:

¾ cup olive oil

¼ cup red wine vinegar, or balsamic vinegar

2 tablespoons water

1 large clove of garlic, smashed

1 teaspoon salt

¼ teaspoon pepper

Pinch of oregano, dried

Pinch of basil, dried

METHOD:

Place all the salad dressing ingredients in a jar or bottle with a good lid. Shake well to blend. Let stand until ready to serve salad. Re-shake bottle and gently pour over greens, mixing well with your hands. Serve immediately.

🌿 *This versatile vegetable can be served as a side dish with just about any meal, or added to a sandwich for a tart, garlicky and olive oil flavor. Serve this salad with good Italian bread, a glass of deep red wine, and you practically have a meal. My mother always made plenty when she cooked this so she would have leftovers to make a quick sandwich or snack. As with all greens, be sure they are soaked, rinsed and drained well before preparing.*

Broccoli Rabe Salad –
Insalata di Cime di Rapa

Serves: 6–8 as a side dish

INGREDIENTS:

2 bunches broccoli rabe, hard stalks trimmed and discarded. Cut stalks and leaves into 2-inch lengths, rinsed and drained well

4–6 cloves garlic, minced

6 tablespoons fresh lemon juice, plus 1 lemon for garnish

4–6 tablespoons olive oil

Salt and ground pepper to taste

Pinch of red pepper flakes or more to taste

METHOD:

Sauté garlic and red pepper flakes in olive oil until garlic is soft. Mix in greens, coat with oil and stir fry for 5–10 minutes.

TO SERVE:

Tastes best at room temperature. Arrange on colorful platter, adding lemon wedges for garnish.

Broccoli Salad – *Insalata di Broccoli*

Serves: 6 as a side dish

INGREDIENTS:

1 bunch fresh broccoli, steamed

2 large lemons, squeezed; 1 additional lemon for garnish

6 cloves garlic, sliced (or see roasted garlic recipe)

½ cup olive oil

Salt and pepper to taste

METHOD:

Wash, drain and slice fresh broccoli. Steam until medium tender – about 5 minutes. Do not overcook! Drain and cool for at least 30 minutes. Combine with garlic, olive oil, lemon juice, salt and pepper, and dress broccoli.

TO SERVE:

Serve on platter with sliced lemon wedges on the side.

VARIATION: My daughter-in-law, Clare Hilger, makes this dish with roasted garlic, which adds a delicious, nutty flavor, as well as a nice golden contrast with the green of the broccoli.

Roasted Garlic

INGREDIENTS:

10 medium heads of garlic

¼ cup olive oil

METHOD:

Cut off the very top of the garlic heads, exposing cloves. Place garlic in a small baking dish. Add olive oil and salt and pepper. Toss to coat. Then turn garlic cloves cut-side up. Cover dish tightly with aluminum foil. Bake in 400° oven until garlic skins are soft and golden brown – approximately 50–60 minutes. Remove and let cool. Squeeze garlic cloves from skin. Slice thinly. Add to broccoli.

Aunt Dolly's Potato Salad – *Insalata di Potate*

Serves: 6

INGREDIENTS:

2 pounds small potatoes (red or Yukon gold)

4 cloves garlic, finely chopped

1 cup celery, diced

½ cup red onion, sliced

1 handful (about ¼ cup) chopped Italian parsley

Olive oil and white wine vinegar, enough to coat potatoes

METHOD:

Boil potatoes in salted water with the skin on until they are tender but still hold their shape. Allow to cool and then peel. Cut into bite-size pieces. Mix garlic, celery, red onions and parsley in a bowl and add potatoes. Pour the olive oil and vinegar mixture over all and gently mix so as to coat everything. Add salt and pepper to taste.

TO SERVE:

If made in advance, remove from refrigerator and let stand a few minutes to take the chill away. Place in a colorful bowl and enjoy.

 My Aunt Dolly, Josephine Castellano Vuocolo, was my father's youngest sister. She was a great aunt, a petite, beautiful woman and a lot of fun. She also was a very good cook, yet didn't receive a lot of attention or credit for her cooking because she was overshadowed by her mother, my Grandma Castellano, who was always in full command of any kitchen. I have great memories of Aunt Dolly. She was very energetic and had a great sense of humor. Her laugh was contagious. She loved her nieces, and she lavished on us with trips and gifts. As Lorrie mentioned, she let us rummage through her closet and drawers trying on her clothes, high-heel shoes and jewelry. She took us to the Jersey shore. She was a sun-worshipper. She was opinionated about politics, locally and nationally, faithful to the Democratic Party, and introduced me to many of the political beliefs and leanings I have to this day. Aunt Dolly could make any simple dish taste special. She had an artistic flair about her, and that showed up in her home décor, in the way she dressed, and in the kitchen. She loved traditional Italian food, yet was equally comfortable trying new recipes.

 Lorrie adds: This potato salad is far superior to the mayo-based kind. It's lighter and you can really taste the potatoes. Aunt Dolly always sliced the potatoes but I prefer cubing them. They're easier to mix and serve. Because of its lightness, it's great to serve in the summer. I always make it on the 4th of July and serve with hamburgers, hot dogs and salad.

Tomato Salad – *Insalata di Pomodoro*

Serves: 4

INGREDIENTS:

5 medium-size, vine-ripened tomatoes

3 cloves garlic chopped

½ small red onion, thinly sliced

10 fresh basil leaves, torn into small pieces

5 fresh oregano leaves or a pinch of dried oregano

⅓ cup olive oil

2 tablespoons balsamic vinegar

2 tablespoons red wine vinegar

A splash of water

Salt and pepper

METHOD:

Slice tomatoes into wedges, making sure you don't crush them and lose their juice. Place tomatoes in a large bowl and sprinkle with salt. Add the garlic, red onion, basil and oregano and mix. In a separate bowl whisk together the olive oil, vinegars and splash of water. Gently dress the salad. Add salt and pepper to taste

TO SERVE:

There are many variations to this salad. In addition to feta or mozzarella, you can add cucumbers, red and green peppers, and black cured olives. Be sure to serve it with a good crunchy Italian or French bread to mop up those delicious juices.

This makes a great lunch sitting outdoors in the summertime, especially if you're lucky enough to be able to pull the tomatoes right off the vine in your own garden. I like to use red onions in this dish, and if I want to make it more substantial, I add balls of mozzarella or a slab of feta cheese. Make extra dressing to dip your bread in. Be sure to be generous with the dressing.

Fennel and Olives – *Finocchio e Olive*

SEE CHAPTER 4 SMALL BITES

Christmas Day Salad – *Insalata di Natale*

Serves: 4

INGREDIENTS:

- 4 oranges, peeled and cut into thin rounds
- 2 small fennel bulbs, trimmed and thinly sliced
- ½ red onion, thinly sliced
- Handful of black olives, preferably black olives cured in oil
- 1 tablespoon balsamic vinegar
- Olive oil to moisten
- Salt to taste
- 1 large clove garlic, peeled and cracked

> *Lorrie found some recipes in her file that our mother had typewritten and sent to her. One of them was a "sort of" recipe. It said: "Our Christmas Day dinner salad when I was a little girl always included slices of California oranges, romaine lettuce and black olives. The dressing had lots of olive oil and salt, and the salad bowl was rubbed with garlic. Wine vinegar was added, and it marinated for about 30 minutes before it was served." What makes this recipe so special is that one time my mother told us that one of the reasons she loved Christmas as a child was because they had oranges to eat. Oranges were not plentiful at that time and were very expensive, according to her, so having them was a real treat. I re-created this recipe, trying to honor my mother's memory of her childhood Christmases.*

METHOD:

Rub garlic clove around the sides and bottom of the salad bowl. Slice top and bottom of oranges and cut away peel and white pith. Carefully cut away membrane. Do this over salad bowl to catch any juice. Place fennel slices, olives and onion in large bowl, add vinegar and enough olive oil to coat the ingredients. Add orange slices and salt gently mix, adding additional olive oil if needed.

TO SERVE:

Let set for 30 minutes before serving. Drizzle with more olive oil if needed.

Chapter 8

❧❧❧❧❧

Pizza

Mom's Pizza – *Pizza alla Marinara*

The most traditional pizza of the Campania region, the birthplace of pizza.

Serves: Makes 2 large pizzas

THE DOUGH:

6 cups flour (approximately)

1 teaspoon salt

1 teaspoon sugar

3 packages of dried yeast

2 cups hot water

2 tablespoons olive oil

Additional olive oil

METHOD:

In mixing bowl, add 2 cups flour, yeast, salt, sugar and mix. Add water and olive oil and beat until thoroughly blended. Let stand until yeast begins to bubble. Add 2 cups of flour and mix with a spatula, adding flour until it forms into a sticky ball. Turn out on a flour-dusted counter or wooden board, adding flour as needed. Keep kneading until the dough is smooth, elastic, and no longer sticks to your hands (approximately 5–8 minutes). You will have to add more flour to the dough and the surface upon which you are kneading it to get it to an elastic, smooth consistency.

Spread olive oil around the sides and bottom of a large pot. Oil dough and place in pot and cover. It will take about 45 minutes to rise. Let it rise, then punch it down and cover and let it rise again.

Michele mixing the yeast and water

Kneading the dough

PIZZA TOPPINGS:

1 pound mozzarella cheese, sliced or grated

2 large handfuls of Parmigiano-Reggiano cheese, grated

2 teaspoons basil, dried

2 teaspoons oregano, dried

Garlic powder, to taste

Salt and pepper, to taste

Olive oil

1 large can tomatoes, crushed, or leftover tomato sauce, heated

PUTTING THE PIZZA TOGETHER:

Divide dough in half. Spread on oiled pizza pans and sprinkle salt, pepper, garlic powder, oregano, basil, mozzarella and Parmigiano-Reggiano cheese and tomato sauce on top. Drizzle olive oil over the tops of the pizzas.

Bake in 475–500° oven for 20 minutes. After the pizzas have baked 10 minutes, switch them from the shelf they are on, so each has 10 minutes on bottom shelf and 10 minutes on top shelf. If bottom of pizzas are not crisp enough, bake a few more minutes.

TO SERVE:

Let pizza cool 5–10 minutes. Then cut slices using kitchen scissors.

Spreading the dough in the film canister

My mother made the best pizza ever. As good a cook as she was, in my mind, her pizza was her greatest culinary accomplishment! Her mother, Camille Salvatoriello Cibella, taught my mother how to make pizza the way her mother in Caposele, Italy, taught her. Aside from Pizza with Anchovies, which she made on Christmas Eve, I do not remember my mother making anything but cheese pizza. One time on Christmas Eve, when she was kneading dough for pizza, she told me that even her mother-in-law didn't know how to make pizza. My mother was so proud of herself knowing she had surpassed her mother-in-law in the kitchen with her pizza-making.

Like Lorrie before me, my mother tried to teach me to make pizza. I had such a hard time because her recipes only included ingredients, not measurements. One day, standing in her kitchen in Houston, I asked her to create a recipe for me that I could understand. While it annoyed her to have to measure as she went, she was pleased that I wanted to learn, so she did it.

I still have my handwritten notes, dated May 7, 1970. I shared them with my son, Jeremy, when he wanted to learn to make pizza, and since then he has created his own way of doing it. I still use my mother's recipe to this day, and it makes enough dough for 2 very large, delicious pizzas. When my mother made pizza, the house would fill up first with that sharp smell of yeast. Later on, when she was stretching the dough in the pan, the scents of basil, oregano and cheese filled the air. While baking in the oven, that delicious fragrance of tomatoes and olive oil came through. Even today, when I make pizza and smell that wonderful aroma, it makes me feel that security and comfort of home and that all is right with the world.

The pans my mother used for her pizza and the way in which she cut the pizza are two things that stand out as unique to her. Because my mother's mother was from Caposele, Italy, a small mountain town outside of Naples, she made pizza Neapolitan-style. It was thick, oily, with a browned crust on the bottom, and scrumptious. It was so thick that it was sometimes a challenge to find pizza pans deep enough. As Lorrie mentioned, my mother discovered that metal film cans (yes, the big round cans that held movie film) were the perfect size and depth. Determined in everything she did, this was no different. She pursued the trail like a true Italian-American and found those film cans. They came to her by way of her uncle's son's neighbor's wife's cousin who worked for a short time in a small film company in New York. My mother managed to secure enough of them to distribute them to a few of us who still carry on the tradition of making her pizza. We use and cherish these pans to this day, and the next generation is already clamoring for them.

Lastly, my mother did not believe in using what is commonly known as a pizza cutter to cut slices of pizza. She cut her pizza with a large, red-handled kitchen scissors made by Swiss. This scissor was the most-used and versatile utensil in her kitchen, and she always referred to it as the "red-handled scissor" because the handles were painted red. After years of use, the red practically disappeared, leaving just a few dots of color, but it was still referred to as the red-handled scissors. My mother used those scissors for many things in the kitchen besides pizza. She snipped parsley, cut chicken parts, trimmed meat and cut the string around the braciole after it was cooked. If one of us dared to use them for cutting paper or anything other than food, you could be sure a scolding would come. Those scissors are still being used today by my brother, Joe.

Lorrie's Pizza

Serves: Makes 1 large pizza

INGREDIENTS:

2 packets of active dry yeast

1 cup warm water

1 tablespoon sugar

3½ cups all-purpose flour

¼ cup olive oil

1 teaspoon salt

½ teaspoon pepper

1 teaspoon chopped fresh rosemary (optional)

1 quart of tomatoes (This is when you'll be happy you canned your own. If you didn't, be sure to buy the best canned tomatoes you can find.)

3 cloves of garlic, finely chopped

A pinch of crushed red pepper or to taste

4 or 5 basil leaves, chopped, plus 4 or 5 left whole and set aside

¼ teaspoon oregano, dried

2 pounds fresh mozzarella cheese sliced ¼-inch thick

Handful of grated parmesan cheese

THE DOUGH:

When making pizza dough it is important that everything you use, utensils included, are warm. Rinse a measuring cup with hot water and fill it to 1 cup. Add the yeast and sugar. Stir with a wooden spoon that has been run under hot water. Set aside so it can bubble up. The top of the yeast should be foamy, and the liquid part cloudy.

In a bowl that has been run under hot water and then dried, add the flour, salt, pepper, olive oil and rosemary, if you're using it. Mix with the warm wooden spoon. Make a well in the center of the flour mixture and add the yeast. Mix until everything is moistened. Then, keeping the mixture in the bowl, start kneading and folding over and kneading some more until everything is combined and the dough is easy to handle – not sticky or too hard. If it's sticky, add a bit of flour. If it's hard, add some olive oil or water.

Lorrie's grandchildren Zazie and Finn make their first pizza and learn a family tradition.

Now you're ready to prepare the dough to rise. In a clean, warm bowl splash some olive oil and roll the dough in it so it's completely coated. Cover the bowl with two or three clean kitchen towels. I use a heating pad set on low to help my dough rise. You can turn your oven on for a few seconds, turn it off and place the covered dough in the oven as well. It will rise in a few hours. When it doubles in size you can make your pizza or punch it down and allow it to rise again. I can never wait that long. One rise is enough for me.

PIZZA TOPPING:

Tomato sauce: Sauté the garlic and crushed red pepper in the olive oil. Add the tomatoes, the basil and oregano and let simmer uncovered so it thickens. In the meantime, slice the mozzarella and grate the Parmesan cheese.

PUTTING THE PIZZA TOGETHER:

On a well-oiled cookie sheet with a lip on it, or a film can if you're lucky enough to find one, place the dough and carefully stretch it towards the corners depending on how thick you like your pizza. When the dough is in place, splash some olive oil on it and, with your hands, spread it around to cover the whole surface. Then place the slices of mozzarella, cover that with the tomato sauce and sprinkle with Parmesan cheese. Place the pizza in an oven that has been preheated to 500° for 20 minutes.

TO SERVE:

Spread the whole basil leaves on the top of the pizza so that each piece you serve has one. As Michele described, the best way to cut a pizza is with a kitchen scissor. Serve with a crunchy green salad and a good red wine.

Mom's Anchovy Pizza – *La Pizza con de Acciughe*

SEE CHAPTER 11 CHRISTMAS EVE

Variation: Anchovy Pizza with Tomato Sauce

Chapter 9

Canning Tomatoes

When I was growing up, many Italian-American women canned their own tomatoes. Tomatoes are such an important staple of the Italian diet. Most Italian families grew their own tomatoes in the backyard, though not in the quantity needed to put up several hundred quarts each year. There was always a "vegetable man" who could procure the best, ripest, reddest tomatoes for his customers when it came time for canning.

My maternal grandfather, Grandpa Tomaso Cibella, always had tomatoes growing in small plots in his tiny backyard. He used whatever sticks he could find to stake them up, and they were planted wherever there was a bit of soil. He also had a fig tree on the edge of his garden. In the winter, he would wrap it up with rags to protect it from the cold. When spring came, he unwrapped it, and it would bloom and produce succulent figs.

As a child, his garden always looked haphazard and messy. I realize today it is because he used every inch of land he had in that miniature backyard for his beloved tomato, hot pepper and basil plants. At the time, I thought that tomatoes must be very precious because they were held in high regard in my family. Now, I realize that they were life-giving to the Italian-American, almost as much as Italian bread.

Tomato canning time always brings back warm memories. The basement in our house in West Orange, New Jersey, had a section with a stove and sink and a long wooden table or counter which was temporarily set up at tomato canning time. Rosie Conforti was always there, and the day she arrived with her little overnight bag in hand I knew there would be a lot of work, laughter, and talking down in the basement. The canning usually took two days, and Rosie spent the night with us so she and my mother would be ready to go to work early in the morning.

I have a few memories of her son, Michael, carrying bushels of tomatoes through the back door of our house, and bringing them down to the basement. Michael had a girlfriend, who he later married, and one time when he was delivering the tomatoes, I was so excited and exclaiming how beautiful they were. Michael was going on about his girlfriend, Roseanne, and how much in love he was with her. He said "Roseanne is my tomato." I was about 8 years old, and that was the first time I ever heard a man refer to a woman like that!

The tomatoes were always filled to the brim in wooden bushels – a natural color bushel basket with green stays in it, and small wire handles on each side to make picking it up easier. And the fragrance – the whole house smelled of fresh tomatoes. My mother and Rosie would set up the huge pots, strainers, wooden spoons, clear glass Ball jars, with a few blue ones in the mix. They were mainly quart size, but some were pint size. There was always a huge stack of fresh wash cloths and dish towels. I was not allowed to help. They thought it was too dangerous for a child because of the huge pots of boiling water. My mother's and Rosie's faces were shiny with the steam of the cooking pots, and they would use their long, front aprons to wipe their faces.

After they canned the tomatoes, they would make "salzine," a word they used for tomato paste. (I tried to find salzine or salzina to which my Mom referred in the recipe, in the Italian/English dictionary, but could not find it. It must be a form of dialect. The Italian words for tomato paste are concentrato di pomodoro). Sometimes they would use tall, skinny bottles in which they placed the cooked paste – almost like a glass soda bottle. There was a special hand-operated capping machine. They used shiny, gold caps, with ridges around the edges, and this machine would crimp the ridges onto the bottle. It was fascinating to watch. Again, I was not allowed to help because they thought it wasn't safe for a child to operate.

In the end, there were 200 or more quarts to last the winter. When the jars would cool, and the flat metal caps would "ping," that meant they had sealed. My mother and Rosie were always happy to hear those sounds. Rosie would stay until the last jar "pinged" and if there were some that didn't, they got thrown away. She and my mother would clean up the basement kitchen area and put the jars in the cellar, which was a small, cool room right near the kitchen area, with a small window in it that could be opened depending on the weather. That is where they were kept stored during the year.

Days later, Rosie would come back with her husband, Frank the Barber, and she would take some canned tomatoes home. She never took as many as my mother wanted her to have. Rosie would say, "Cleo (my mother's nickname), you have more kids to feed than I have."

My sister Lorrie and brother Joe still carry on the family tradition of canning tomatoes every year, and they are every bit as tasty as the ones my mother and her dear friend Rosie canned all those years ago.

The canning tomato story would not be complete without mentioning a little something about Frank Conforti, Rosie's husband. He was a barber, and, in the Italian tradition, he was always known as "Frank the Barber" or "The Barber." He cut the hair of my sisters, brother and me. This was always a great trauma for me because "The Barber" only knew one type of girl's haircut called "The Shingle." It was a haircut that was very short in the back – almost shaved – and longer on the sides and top.

We'd go to their house in Bloomfield, New Jersey, and go down to their basement where Frank had a little barbershop set up. He had what seemed like an enormous barber's chair, complete with black leather seat, black padded back and arm rests, and a long brown leather strap hanging off the side of the chair, which he used to sharpen a razor when he was giving someone a shave. The chair had giant stainless steel hardware on it, and some type of white porcelain trim. It was scary to me as a child, especially seeing that leather strap. He had a wooden booster board that was padded in the same black covering as the chair, and he placed it over the arm rests. I would then climb up to it so I'd be high enough for him to reach me. Every haircut from "The Barber" made me cry. I begged him not to give me "The Shingle," and my mother always told him to do it anyway, which he did.

In spite of the haircuts, it was hard to dislike "The Barber," however, because he was always smiling and joking around and calling his wife Rosie his "Black Beauty," which was so amusing to me. Rosie had olive skin and thick jet-black hair, and a beautiful round face, and she always wore bright pink lipstick and penciled in her eyebrows to make them appear darker and fuller. He would tell my mother and father how beautiful my sisters and I were. He'd say, "These Castellano girls are all beauties, just beauties." Looking back, he was quite a character. Sometimes while my mother and Rosie were canning tomatoes, I'd quietly sit on the basement stairs watching them until they seemed to forget I was there. I would hear Rosie complaining about the Barber – that he gambled away their savings, or that he spent money on flashy clothes. I would overhear snippets of my mother confiding to Rosie about my father's family and the demands they made on her. When my mother noticed me, she would shoo me away.

One last note about Rosie: When I was 13 years old, I was invited to a high school prom by one of our neighbors in West Orange, New Jersey. The only reason I was allowed to say yes was because my parents knew the boy and his family very well. I was both scared and excited. I remember wondering what I was supposed to wear. Rosie happened to be at our house when the invitation came, and she asked my mother about it. Being the always frugal one, my mother said she was hoping I could wear a gown that belonged to one of my older sisters. Rosie wouldn't hear of it. She immediately swung into action, telling my mother about a shop she knew in New York City where I could get a beautiful gown for very little money.

A few days later, my mother, Rosie and I went to New York. I do not remember the trip, whether we drove or took the train, but I do remember the store. It was a tiny place on a crowded, narrow street that was filled with gowns of all styles, sizes and colors. There was hardly a place to stand because there were so many gowns. Rosie went through the racks, pulling out dresses and inspecting them. The only one I tried on was the one we bought.

That dress was beautiful. It was my very first "grown-up" dress. It was a white organza, knee-length gown, with spaghetti straps (because the nuns at the Catholic high school where the prom was to be held would not allow strapless gowns) and had bright colored embroidered flowers on the bodice and on the skirt of the dress. Some of the stems and leaves of the flowers were a bright, almost apple green, and even today when I see that color, I think of that dress. We then went to a shoe store, and I picked out a pair of white satin two-and-one-half-inch heels that had pointy toes – my first pair of "high-heel" shoes. Rosie paid for the dress and shoes. She suggested that I wear my hair in a French twist, which my hairdresser cousin, Johanna Stefanelli Andolora, did for me. I thought I looked like a princess. I have no memory of my date, the prom or whether I had a good time or not. But, I do remember Rosie and that dress!

Mom's Canned Tomatoes

I have two recipes from my mother on how to can tomatoes, one written by her on an index card and another typed by her on a scrap of paper. The index card said: "Use fresh, firm, sound ripe tomatoes. Wash, clean before scalding. Scald to loosen skins, then dip into cool water. Cut out all core and green spots. Skin, pack and process immediately. Pack the whole or cut tomatoes tightly into hot fruit jars. Press each layer to release enough juice to fill spaces between tomatoes. Add 1 teaspoon salt to each quart. Adjust cap according to instructions. Process 45 minutes in boiling water bath."

LORRIE ADDS:

I can't believe this is my mother's recipe for canning tomatoes, a process that requires what seems like a million steps, boiled down to a small index card. Just like her to make it seem simple. I've been canning tomatoes for almost 20 years, and I have a "Rosie," my good friend, Bonnie Anderson. Every year we can over 300 pounds of tomatoes. One year, because all our friends wanted to learn, we canned 500 pounds over two days. Bonnie made us both sign a contract saying we'd never do that again! Here are the directions that we wrote as we canned back in 2005. They're good directions. We haven't poisoned anyone yet!

Lorrie's Canned Tomatoes – *The Complete Recipe*

Serves: 300 pounds makes approximately 150 quarts of tomatoes

INGREDIENTS:

300 pounds of organic ripe tomatoes

1 box Kosher salt

2 bunches organic basil

When summer comes, we start thinking of tomatoes, hundreds of pounds of tomatoes. We spend hours – no, days – canning enough tomatoes to last all winter for our families, including grown children and their families. Lately my brother, Joe, and his family have joined us.

In August we make a trip to the farmer's market to talk to our favorite farmer, Judy, who manages Molina Creek Farm in Davenport, California. We check in with her about how the crop is doing. She grows organic dry farmed tomatoes. That means the tomatoes are not regularly watered so they pull all their flavor from mother earth. They are meaty and as sweet as candy. Because canning is such a labor intensive project, the tomatoes you choose are important. Do a tasting test at your local farmer's market and choose the variety you like.

Through the years, we've canned from 50 pounds to 500. We've found that 300 pounds is a good amount for two people willing to spend a weekend in a labor of love. It's worth it when the tomatoes in the grocery stores are pink and hard and flavorless to be able to reach into the pantry and pull out a taste of summer. Our tomatoes make every recipe in this book taste better.

When Judy says the tomatoes in the field are ready, we put in our order. We can often get what's called "canning tomatoes" which are not perfect and are ripe so the price is usually less. Plus ordering 300 pounds usually comes with a discount.

METHOD:

The day before gather together the following items:

1. Jars, domes and lids: Two pounds of tomatoes make one quart. So you'll need half the number of jars as pounds you're planning to can. For example, for 80 pounds, you'll need 40 quart jars. Purchase jars, domes and lids at your local hardware store or supermarket. Run the jars through a hot cycle on your dishwasher. Place them on the kitchen counter and cover them with clean dish towels.

2. One large 24-quart pot: this is used to boil water to blanch the tomatoes to loosen the skins.

3. One canner with rack: this is for the 45-minute "bath" to seal the tomato jars.

4. One 7-inch, long-handled strainer for placing the tomatoes in the boiling water and retrieving them.

5. One large bowl of cold water to dip the tomatoes in after they are blanched to help further loosen the skin.

6. One sharp paring knife for cutting out the core and any green or damaged parts on the tomato.

7. One jar carrier to safely place jars in the boiling "bath" and retrieving them. You can find all of these items in a good hardware store.

Lorrie scalding the tomatoes

Bonnie skinning the tomatoes

Wiping the rim

Putting jars in the bath

Now you're ready to go!

1. Arrive at the farmer's market early to pick up your pre-ordered tomatoes. Buy a bunch or two of organic basil.
2. Put about 18 quarts of water in your 24-quart pot and bring to a boil. While waiting for the water to boil, line up your clean quart jars. Place one teaspoon salt and a sprig of washed basil in each jar.
3. Wash the tomatoes by dunking them in a bowl of water to get rid of dust and dirt. We use a garden hose and a large bucket, and we do it in the back yard.
4. When the water is boiling, put two strainers full of tomatoes into the boiling water for about one minute or less. The smaller the tomatoes, the shorter the time they'll need for the skin to wrinkle. When this happens, using the strainer, retrieve the tomatoes and place them in a bowl of cold water.
5. Using your paring knife, take out the top of the core and, holding the skin, squeeze out the tomato directly into one of the quart jars. Fill each jar to within 1½ inches

from the top. You'll need to push the tomatoes down to fill all the space in the jar. Use your knife to do this and to get air bubbles out.

6. Repeat until all jars are filled.

Now you're ready to prepare the jars for the bath. This is the process that seals the jars and allows them to remain fresh all winter.

1. With a fresh cloth wipe the glass rim of each jar so that it's clean. Place a dome on the clean mouth and screw on the lid. The lid should be tight enough to hold the dome in place so that it seals properly.

2. Put your canner with the rack on to boil. Water will need to be deep enough to cover your quart jars by 1 to 2 inches. Once the water is boiling, place a quart jar in each section of the rack. Lower the rack into the water and boil for 45 minutes.

3. Remove the jars from the "bath," place them away from drafts and cover them so they cool slowly. We use an old quilt to cover the jars.

Now all you have to do is wait for the "pings." As each jar seals, it lets out a little sound that, after all this work, is music to your ears.

1. The next morning, check all jars. They are sealed if the dome is sucked down and concave. Unscrew the lids, leaving the domes in place and store your tomatoes in a cool dry place away from sunlight. If you have any that haven't sealed, pour the contents in a freezer bag and either freeze or use within a couple of days.

TO SERVE:

Open a bottle of wine and put the pasta on.

Allowing jars to cool down slowly

Time for a little pasta and a glass of wine

Chapter 10

Everyday Meals
i Pasta di Tutti i Giorni

Mom's Polenta – *Migliacchio*

Serves: 6

INGREDIENTS:

6 cups water

2 teaspoons salt

1¾ cups of course ground corn meal

METHOD:

Bring the salted water to a boil. Pour in the cornmeal slowly and gradually, stirring constantly so it doesn't form lumps. Lower the heat so it simmers and continue to stir. It will take about 20 minutes. It should be creamy and coarse at the same time.

TO SERVE:

Serve it topped with marinara sauce or sautéed broccoli rabe or other greens and a handful of parmesan cheese.

> *My mother loved polenta, but she didn't make it often because as children some of us didn't like it. Later on, when most of us had left home, she would make it more often. I can still see her standing over a large pot, stirring the polenta very fast with a large wooden spoon. She said if you left the polenta for a minute, it would ruin it. She was like a marathon runner with this dish – she could produce great results in a hurry.*
>
> *This is a good time to mention the wooden spoons in my mother's kitchen. She always used them while cooking practically every dish you can think of. Her wooden spoons were large, very dark brown in color or even had burn marks on them. They were versatile tools used also for discipline. "I'm going to get the wooden spoon," she'd threaten when we misbehaved. And when she did, her aim was good, and it always hurt!*
>
> **Lorrie Adds:** *When we were growing up, we had a piano teacher, Mrs. Guerino, who came to the house every Saturday morning to teach all of us kids plus my father to play the piano. Since lessons finished right about lunch time, she was often invited to stay and eat with us. Mom made polenta with marinara sauce. I remember those lunches because the yellow of the polenta and the red of the sauce offended my esthetics. I just thought red and yellow didn't go together. But it was so good, I ate it anyway.*

Lentil Soup

This recipe can be very versatile, and you can add, once again, "what you have." If my mother wanted to "stretch it" (an expression my mother used when she was afraid she didn't have enough prepared, which was unusual), she might add peeled, chopped potatoes, rice, or any tiny pasta such as orzo.

Serves: 6

INGREDIENTS:

2 cups dry lentils, rinsed. Discard any very dark lentils.

5 cups water

2 carrots, peeled and cut into ½-inch rounds

2 stalks celery, chopped

½ onion, chopped

½ tablespoon basil, dried

⅛ teaspoon oregano, dried

½ cup olive oil

Salt and pepper

METHOD:

Sauté carrots, celery and onion in olive oil. Add lentils, water, basil, oregano, salt and pepper. Bring to a boil and then simmer for 2 hours.

TO SERVE:

Serve with Italian bread and a green salad.

LORRIE ADDS:

When cooking this dish with my mother, she always added a half cup of olive oil to the finished soup, saying it gave it more body and flavor. Who can argue with that, a half cup of olive oil to anything would improve it!

Eggplant Parmigiana

> This is a time-consuming dish, but my mother loved it so much she didn't mind that it took a while to make. I watched my mother make it so often while growing up that I have the recipe committed to memory. She usually served it with thick-cut Italian bread. And, when it was served as a leftover, it made a great sandwich.
>
> This is the perfect time to mention what a sandwich lover my mother was. My father always said she could make a sandwich out of anything, including sautéed spinach, broccoli rabe, stuffed cherry peppers or roasted peppers – just give her a good loaf of Italian bread.

Eggplant Parmigiana Sandwich

Mom's Eggplant Parmigiana – *Parmigiana di Melanzane*

Serves: 4–6

INGREDIENTS:

1 large eggplant, peeled, leaving on small lines of skin

4 eggs, beaten with a little milk

2 cups flour

2 cups bread crumbs

1 pound mozzarella cheese, sliced or coarsely grated

2 cups Parmigiano-Reggiano cheese, grated

1 large can of crushes tomatoes, or left-over tomato sauce

Olive oil

Salt and pepper

METHOD:

Peel and slice eggplant in rounds. Place in colander in layers, salting each layer. Cover with heavy dish and let stand about 30 minutes to drain out any bitterness. Wipe eggplant slices with fresh kitchen towel or paper towels.

Dip each eggplant slice in flour, then egg mixture, then bread crumbs. Heat olive oil. Sauté eggplant until golden brown, draining on paper towels or brown paper bags.

Place large spoonful of tomato sauce in a large baking dish, layer bottom of dish with eggplant rounds, cover with thin layer of both cheeses, top with thin layer of tomato sauce and salt and ground pepper. Continue to layer – should make about 3 layers. Top with cheeses and sauce. Cover with aluminum foil. Bake at 350° for 45 minutes or until sauce is bubbling. Let stand about 15 minutes before cutting into serving pieces.

TO SERVE:

Italian bread and a salad go with this perfectly.

Aunt Rose's Menest' and Beans – Minestra or Escarole and Beans

This hearty dish is especially good to eat when the weather begins to turn cool. It warms the heart and soul. My mother and Aunt Rose Cibella loved this dish. In those days, there was no such thing as pre-washed greens. As Lorrie mentioned, they were particular about washing greens very well to remove sand and soil. They soaked the greens and then carefully lifted them out of the large soaking bowl so as not to disturb the sand and soil that had fallen to the bottom. This was done three or four times, changing the water, until the water was clear.

Serves: 4

INGREDIENTS:

2 large heads of escarole

1 can cannellini beans

1 teaspoon basil, dried

2 cloves garlic, chopped

2 or 3 tablespoons olive oil

Salt and pepper

METHOD:

One at a time, lay each head of escarole on its side and cut every 2 inches until you get to the core. Discard the core. Soak in a bowl of cold water and lift the escarole leaves out of the water directly into a large pot to steam, using only the water that remains on the leaves. Salt the escarole to taste. Simmer covered until the leaves become wilted and are tender, about 10 minutes. Try not to lift the cover during this process because you'll lose the green color of the leaves.

In a smaller sauce pan add the olive oil and garlic and sauté until garlic is soft. Add can of beans and the bean juices to the olive oil and garlic. Add the basil. With a fork or potato masher, mash about half the beans so there is a creamy sauce along with the whole beans. Simmer for 2 or 3 minutes. Pour the beans directly into the escarole pot and let simmer for a few minutes so that the flavors mix. Taste and correct seasoning.

TO SERVE:

Serve with a salad and good crunchy bread to dip into the broth.

❦ **Lorrie says:** *However you say it, it's another one of those delicious comfort foods we had growing up. We called it Jambought. That's how it was pronounced. The dialect from southern Italy was a spoken language, so I guess we don't have to worry about spelling it correctly.*

Jambought/Jambota/Ciambotta

Serves: 6

INGREDIENTS:

4 tablespoons olive oil

3 cloves garlic, crushed

1 onion, cut in half and then thinly sliced

1 green pepper, thickly sliced and cut into 1-inch pieces

1 pound zucchini, cut into ½-inch rounds

10 small white or Yukon potatoes

1 pound string beans, remove the ends and snap in half

1 quart tomatoes

2 tablespoons basil, fresh, or 1 teaspoon basil, dried

¼ teaspoon oregano, dried

METHOD:

Parboil the potatoes until they are cooked but not too soft. Let cool and cut into bite-size pieces. Save the potato water. Parboil the string beans for about 4 minutes. Drain and save the string bean water. Heat the oil in a large soup pot. Sauté the garlic and onions until soft but not brown. Add the peppers and sauté for a few minutes. Add the rest of the ingredients along with a total of 2 cups of the saved string bean and potato water. Season with salt and pepper to taste. Bring to a boil and simmer until all the vegetables are cooked.

TO SERVE:

This is a very satisfying but light stew. For added flavor make it in the morning or the night before and let it sit so the flavors really mix. Leftovers make a great lunch or side dish for the next day's dinner.

Aunt Rose's Spinach and Potatoes

Serves: 4

INGREDIENTS:

2 pounds spinach, washed and cut into 2-inch to 3-inch pieces

1 pound Yukon or small red potatoes

3 cloves garlic, chopped

Salt and pepper

Scant ¼ cup olive oil

METHOD:

Parboil potatoes so they can be pierced with a fork but not fall apart. Then cut into bite-size pieces. Skin can be left on or peeled depending on your preference.

Sauté garlic in olive oil. When garlic is soft but not brown, add spinach and potatoes. Sauté for 15 minutes so that flavors mix and spinach is cooked. Add reserved potato water as needed. Add salt and pepper to taste.

TO SERVE:

This makes a great light dinner or a hearty lunch with a salad and Italian bread.

Aunt Rose's String Beans and Potatoes

Serves: 6

INGREDIENTS:

2 pounds string beans with ends removed, washed, and snapped in half

1 pound small red or Yukon potatoes, peeled or with skin

1 large onion, cut in half and thinly sliced

2 cloves garlic, chopped

1 tablespoons basil, dried, or 2 tablespoons chopped fresh basil

¼ teaspoon oregano, dried

1 quart crushed tomatoes

Scant ¼ cup olive oil

METHOD:

String beans: parboil for 4 minutes, drain and set aside. Potatoes: Parboil until a fork pierces them, but they don't fall apart, peel (optional). Drain and cut into bite-size pieces.

Sauté onion and garlic in olive oil until soft. Combine green beans, potatoes, tomatoes, basil and oregano with the onion and garlic. Simmer for 20 minutes. Add salt and pepper to taste.

TO SERVE:

Just add a green salad and Italian bread for a light, tasty meal.

Mena's Peppers and Eggs

Serves: 4

INGREDIENTS:

3 large bell peppers – green, red, yellow, or whatever you have, diced

½ small onion, chopped

6 eggs

4 tablespoons olive oil

Pinch of oregano, dried

1 tablespoon fresh basil, chopped, or 1 teaspoon dried basil

1 tablespoon fresh Italian parsley, chopped

Salt and pepper

METHOD:

Heat the oil in a heavy frying pan. Add peppers and onions and sauté until they are barely soft. Add basil, parsley, and oregano. Beat the eggs with salt and pepper and add them to the peppers and onions. When the edges of the eggs pull away from the sides of the pan, and the bottom is lightly browned, it's time to turn it over and lightly brown the other side.

TO SERVE:

This dish makes a great sandwich or a good breakfast.

LORRIE ADDS:

My sister Mena makes the best peppers and eggs. She uses a combination of red, green and yellow peppers for a colorful effect. The secret to great peppers and eggs is plenty of olive oil. Don't skimp on it. If you're watching calories, this is not the place to do it. You can make this dish in a regular frying pan, but for best results use two frying pans that can be hooked together for easy turning. Mena sometimes throws in a chopped, hot spicy pepper. This dish can also be made as a scrambled egg dish if you don't have the equipment to turn it over.

VARIATION:

Substitute potatoes for the peppers, and you have Potatoes and Eggs, or add potatoes to the peppers for Potatoes, Peppers and Eggs.

Sausage and Peppers

Serves: 6

INGREDIENTS:

¼ cup olive oil

6 links Italian pork sausage

1 of each red, green, yellow bell peppers, sliced

2 yellow onions, sliced

½ teaspoon oregano, dried

1 tablespoon basil, dried

4 cloves of garlic, finely chopped

¼ teaspoon red pepper flakes (optional)

METHOD:

In a large frying pan, heat the oil. Add the sausages and cook until brown on all sides. Remove from the pan. Set aside. Sauté the garlic in the same oil as the sausage. When it is soft add the peppers, onions, oregano, basil, salt and pepper. Sauté until golden brown. Add the sausage to the pan and stir to combine. Cook about 20 minutes so that the sausages are cooked through.

TO SERVE:

This makes a delicious, filling sandwich on crunchy torpedo-shaped rolls. For dinner, serve with broccoli rabe or potato salad.

LORRIE ADDS:

When my sister Gina got married, the family flew to Houston to celebrate. The night before the wedding reception, we made this dish. Everyone had something to say about how to make it. There were eight cooks, and this is one time that "too many cooks didn't spoil the broth." We had so much fun arguing about who made it best and who Mom gave the real recipe to. This is our legacy. Our mother, in her creativity, gave all of us a slightly different one. The one here is mine, and I claim its authenticity because my mother's recipe tastes like the Sausage and Peppers from La Fest'. At least that's my story.

Settlement House Meatloaf

Serves: 6–8

INGREDIENTS:

1½ pounds ground beef

1 cup milk

1 tablespoon Worcestershire sauce

½ teaspoon salt

½ teaspoon ground mustard

¼ teaspoon pepper

1 egg

3 slices white bread (practically unheard of in our house!), finely chopped

1 small onion, chopped

½ cup ketchup

METHOD:

Mix all ingredients together except ketchup. Spread mixture in ungreased loaf pan. Spread ketchup on top. Bake uncovered at 350° for 1 hour to 1¼ hours. Drain meatloaf drippings. Let stand 5 minutes. Remove from pan and cut into thick slices.

TO SERVE:

Serve with broccoli salad.

My interest in food and cooking has been a part of me since I was a little girl. When I was about 10 years old, I wanted to learn to make meatloaf. Many of my friends in grade school were not Italian, and I noticed that they ate meatloaf for supper or had meatloaf sandwiches for lunch. It was the 1950s, and the Betty Crocker Cookbook was the Bible for many of my friend's mothers, but not mine. I asked my mother to teach me how to make it.

"Why do you want to make that?" Derogatory emphasis on "that."

"I don't make meatloaf. I make meatballs." Superior emphasis on "balls."

I insisted. My mother enrolled me in a class at the Valley Settlement House in West Orange, New Jersey. This was a very unusual thing for her to do because she kept her children close to home. The Settlement House was about eight blocks from home, and I walked to it once a week after school.

The Valley Settlement House is still there, in the same location, only in a new building and now part of the United Way. The classes offered today are different than in the 1950s. They now offer child care, pre-school, literacy classes, and community outreach. The class I took was more like a homemaking class for young girls. We were taught simple things, such as how to hand sew a hem, how to sew a button on a shirt, how to sew a straight hem on a sewing machine, the proper way to wash dishes, ways to maintain a clean home, personal hygiene, and basic cooking skills. Best of all, in our cooking class, we were taught how to make meatloaf.

Settlement Houses were started in the early 1900s to help newly-arrived immigrants learn American social and cultural ways and to help them assimilate into American life. By the 1950s they evolved into community centers and offered what might be called "life skills classes." It was located in an old neighborhood, with small houses in disrepair and a few storefronts. It was staffed by older female teachers and social workers who were friendly and skilled. I recognized that some of the girls in my class were poor, mainly by the way they dressed.

One of the girls I met was named Elizabeth. She wore the same dress every time she came to class. It wasn't starched and ironed like my dress. Her hair was not combed, and the other girls made fun of her. One day at the end of class, I asked my mother if I could give Elizabeth a dress of mine because her dress was so worn. My closet was pretty empty and our clothes budget was small so I was surprised that my mother said yes. I went to Elizabeth's house after class. It was a two-story tenement in Orange, New Jersey. I stood at the bottom of the narrow dark wooden stairs and called her name, "Elizabeth," and she came down and I gave her the dress. It was a deep yellow colored dress, with a white lace trim around the collar and the sleeves. I didn't realize that my gift might be embarrassing to her, but she thanked me, ran up the stairs, and we never saw each other again. Looking back, Elizabeth seemed so alone and uncared for. I recognized in her a feeling of aloneness that I sometimes experienced as a child. Even though I lived with a large family, there wasn't always the notice or attention I desired or needed. I gave to Elizabeth what I desired for myself.

Learning to make meatloaf turned out to be a valuable experience. It was there that I learned how to safely handle a knife, how to slice and chop, how to use measuring spoons and cups, how to light an oven (it was a gas oven and the pilot light had to be manually lit with a match), how to safely place a pan on a hot stove with the handle positioned away from me, and how to set a timer for proper cooking time. These were skills my mother had, but when I was a young girl, she rarely let me near the stove, she rarely measured or timed anything, and she certainly would not let me handle a knife, a hot pan, or a match!

My mother, like other Italian-American women, was fearful and superstitious. She acted as if there was always some invisible harm or evil lurking about. It was a dark view of the world. It's hard to remember a time upon leaving the house when my mother didn't warn me to "be careful." Even in her old age, when my mother would say goodbye to me after a visit, she always ended not with an "I love you," but with "Be careful."

The message that the world is not a safe place was a constant in my childhood. A legacy of Italian culture and poverty must have enhanced the possibility that disaster was just around the corner, and that the "other shoe was waiting to drop." The author, Maria Laurino, addressed this in her book, Old World Daughter, New World Mother, that food plus fear equals Italian mothers. Laurino used the term, "Mamma del Sud," to identify the Italian mother from the southern part of Italy, who was preoccupied with protecting her children from the unseen, which was always considered bad, and to be avoided at all cost. I remember sayings such as, "knock on wood" when something good happened and you hoped it would last, or "God forbid," when you were afraid something bad might happen, or "God willing," when you wanted something that you thought you might not get. My father's response to anything that happened that was unwanted, disappointing or disastrous was, "What are you going to do? You can't do anything." The idea that success or any other good thing was pretty much determined by forces outside our control was underlying. Even the Catholic sign of the cross was used to protect oneself or one's family from a feared or impending disaster – as if to cross out any harm that might come.

These things surely had roots in the ancient Italian belief in the "evil eye," or as Italians say "mal'occhio" (or in southern Italian dialect, "maloyke"). The belief that the world was not safe ended with the stated truth that you were only safe in the family. Anyone else was considered a "stranger" and not to be trusted. My Aunt Dolly looked at anyone who was not a Castellano (her family name) as an outsider. In-laws, who had married into the family for more than 20 years, were still considered strangers according to her. I was frequently reminded, "Blood is thicker than water." The belief that life was not safe also meant that happiness was fleeting, as in "Enjoy it while you can," or that success might be illusive and you better remember, "God helps those who help themselves." Generations of Italian Catholicism, superstition and poverty all contributed to this type of thinking.

My mother was suspicious and psychic. She would have dreams or feelings that would come true. Oftentimes, she would casually predict what was going to happen in a situation, and it did! My father used to shudder and tell us to hope that she never dreamed about us! As if to say that all my mother's dreams were scary and bad. I do think my mother was very intuitive, along with protective and superstitious, which was characteristic of those with the same southern Italian roots and culture from which she came.

As for the meatloaf, I only made it once for my family. I remember how proud I was of myself for making and serving such a different dish. I felt very grown up. I don't recall anyone else's reaction to the meal. Years later, I made meatloaf when my son, Jeremy, was growing up. After my parents were retired, my mother made meatloaf for my father every once in a while. Times had changed.

Aunt Rose's Chicken and Potatoes

Serves: 6

INGREDIENTS:

6 pieces of chicken, skin on

1 large yellow onion, cut in half and sliced

4 cloves finely chopped garlic

3 large potatoes, peeled, cut in half lengthwise and sliced

¼ cup olive oil

1 teaspoon salt and pepper to taste

1 package frozen peas or a can of peas (optional)

METHOD:

Preheat oven to 425°. Place all ingredients in a large bowl and mix so they are well coated. Bake uncovered in a 9-inch-by-13-inch oven-proof dish for 40 minutes. During the last 10 minutes mix in the peas.

TO SERVE:

This is an all-in-one dish. Just add a glass of wine.

Veal Cutlets

Serves: 4

INGREDIENTS:

4 veal cutlets

1 cup all-purpose flour

1 cup bread crumbs

2 eggs, beaten

4 tablespoons olive oil

2 lemons, cut in halves

Salt and pepper

METHOD:

Place each veal cutlet between two sheets of plastic wrap and pound until thin. Mix flour, salt and pepper together and place in a shallow plate. Beat the eggs and place in a shallow bowl. Place the bread crumbs in a shallow plate. Dredge each veal cutlet one at a time first through the flour, then the eggs, and finally the breadcrumbs so they are well coated. Set aside.

Heat the olive oil in a heavy skillet. When the oil is hot, place one or two cutlets in the skillet at a time. Fry slowly until golden brown, about 4 to 6 minutes. Turn over and fry the other side until it, too, is golden brown.

TO SERVE:

Serve on warm plates with half a lemon on each plate to squeeze over the cutlets. Serve with broccoli or tomato salad.

Peas and Pasta

SEE CHAPTER 6 PASTA

Fusilli, Ziti or Cavatelli with broccoli or cauliflower

SEE CHAPTER 6 PASTA

Pasta e Fagioli – *also called Pasta 'Fazool'*

SEE CHAPTER 6 PASTA

Cecida and Pasta – *Chickpeas and Pasta*

SEE CHAPTER 6 PASTA

Chapter 11

CHRISTMAS EVE
The Feast of the Seven Fishes

Christmas Eve dinner was and still is a special event in Italian-American homes. Traditionally known as "The Feast of the Seven Fishes," it is a holiday celebrated when no meat is eaten, in the Catholic tradition of long ago. When we were growing up, sometimes my mother shortened it to Five Fishes. Christmas Eve and Christmas Day were always celebrated at home, with my mother and my Grandma Castellano doing the cooking. On both days, my father's family, the Castellanos, came to our house to celebrate the holidays.

Christmas Eve dinner brought what seemed like many unique foods and aromas to our house. It carried with it the general excitement of the holidays, and a houseful of at least 20 family members. The dining room table was opened up to capacity, and the children's table set up. Both of these tables were covered with the traditional foods.

My mother always set a beautiful table, but Christmas Eve brought out her decorative flair. Crisply ironed white embroidered tablecloths, white linen napkins to match, silver flatware, "Desert Rose" Franciscan pottery, and delicate crystal glasses etched with flowers. (My brother, Joe, and my sister-in-law, Elizabeth Horn Castellano, still have and use these dishes, glasses and linens.) There were always candles on the table, yet I never remember flowers on the table because it was always laden with platters and platters of food. My mother would direct us as to how she wanted the table set. My older sisters would organize us into making place cards for each family member. Sometimes they would be elaborate, like decorating them with Christmas balls and writing each person's name in white, spray "snow." One time, we painted clear glasses with flowers and each person's name on them. Other times, the place cards would be made out of colorful paper, artistically cut and embellished. Each year they would be unique, and everyone looked forward to seeing what we came up with. My Aunt Mena and Aunt Dolly, who thought we were always brilliant, sang our praises no matter the outcome.

My mother was so devoted to carrying out this tradition that she even prepared elaborate Christmas holiday dinners four days before my brother, Joe, was born. Amazing! My mother and grandmother spent hours in the kitchen cleaning and slicing squid, peeling and deveining shrimp, soaking and slicing salted cod fish, (baccala), cleaning smelts, preparing conch, soaking anchovies, preparing peppers, mushrooms and artichokes to be stuffed, cooking fresh broccoli, washing and slicing fresh fennel and pitting black olives for salad, chopping the numerous ingredients for antipasto, mixing pizza dough and all the other ingredients that went into making this meal so special.

As an adult, I carried on the tradition under my mother's careful eye (after she no longer prepared extensive meals such as this) and passed this onto my family.

Christmas Eve Menu

Small Bites
Antipasto
Stuffed Mushrooms
Stuffed Hot & Sweet Cherry Peppers
Fennel & Olives
(See Chapter 4 for all)

Pizza
Tomato & Cheese Pizza
(See Chapter 8)

Anchovy Pizza

Pasta
Cappellini & Anchovies

Fishes
Baccala
Scungelli
Shrimp
Smelts

Salads
Stuffed Artichokes
(See Chapter 4)

Broccoli
(See Chapter 7)

Mom's Anchovy Pizza – *La Pizza con de Acciughe*

Serves: Makes one pizza

INGREDIENTS:

1 large tin of flat anchovies in olive oil

1 cup or more Parmigiano-Romano cheese, grated

½ jar cured calamata olives, pitted

Cracked pepper to taste

Garlic powder to taste

Olive oil

METHOD:

Prepare Mom's Pizza dough recipe and spread in pan. Sprinkle dough with garlic powder and pepper. Cover with Parmigiano-Romano cheese, top with anchovies, and olives, cracked pepper, and garlic powder. Drizzle top with olive oil and the oil left from the anchovy tin. Bake in 450° oven for 10 minutes. Watch this carefully so it doesn't over bake. Remove when bottom of pizza is crispy.

TO SERVE:

Let pizza cool for about 5 minutes. Cut slices using scissors.

Anchovy and Olive Pizza

Cappellini & Anchovies – *Cappellini e Acciughe*

Serves: 4

INGREDIENTS:

1 pound cappellini

½ cup olive oil

8 large cloves garlic, minced

2 cans flat anchovy fillets (2 ounces), drained, chopped

2 teaspoons fresh lemon juice

½ cup fresh Italian flat leaf parsley, chopped

Ground pepper, to taste

METHOD:

Heat olive oil over low heat, add garlic, and cook 2 minutes. Add anchovies and cook until anchovies begin to melt and garlic just about begins to color. Cook cappellini and drain well. Return to pot and add anchovy mixture and lemon juice. Toss well to coat cappellini. Top with ground pepper and sprinkle with parsley. Serve immediately.

TO SERVE:

Place in rimmed bowls, topping with additional parsley.

VARIATION:

For a heartier taste, add 10–12 black oil-cured olives, pitted and chopped, and 2 tablespoons capers in salt, rinsed.

This is one of my favorite dishes of the Christmas Eve meal. As a child, I didn't like it, yet my mother's philosophy of insisting that each of her children "try a little bit" of food that seemed foreign or strange to us (not only anchovies but other foods too) has served us well. Being encouraged to tasting new foods created a mind-set of openness, of willingness to try something new, of being alive to the possibilities that food offered. If the taste was not appealing, it was okay. The important thing is that we tried it and then decided for ourselves. Although I was not aware of it at the time, this cultivated in me a sense of adventure with food and also discouraged an attitude of strong dislikes. To this day, there are few foods that I dislike, and even in the disliking, it's mild. In insisting that we "try a little bit" my mother taught us to respect food and to recognize that there is value in all foods. Italian-Americans believe that food is life. My mother reinforced that belief in this way.

My mother always made this right before serving because she said it would dry out easily. Everyone would be assembled at the table before the dishes of pasta were served, usually by my sisters and me.

Salted Cod Fish – *Baccala*

Serves: 8–10 as side dish

INGREDIENTS:

2 pounds salted cod fish

Olive oil

2 cloves garlic, minced

Italian flat leaf parsley, 1 bunch chopped

1 fresh lemon

Black olives for garnish (optional)

METHOD:

After 48 hours of repeated soaking and draining and changing the water often, drain and place baccala in a pan of boiling water and simmer for about 5 minutes. Drain and set aside to cool. Flake the baccala with a fork, making small pieces. Add olive oil, fresh, chopped Italian parsley, minced garlic and lemon juice to taste. Mix well and chill.

TO SERVE:

This looks great served on a black dish. It can be garnished with black olives and additional chopped Italian parsley and lemon wedges.

Draining the baccala

This dish is served cold and requires 48 hours preparation time. Salted cod fish has to be soaked in water, with water changes frequently to remove most of the salt. It is best to purchase it three days in advance.

One year I arrived in New York the day before Christmas Eve. My son, Jeremy, picked me up at LaGuardia Airport and we went directly from the airport to shop for the ingredients for Christmas Eve dinner. Our first stop was the seafood store "P Zollo & Sons Inc." on Metropolitan Avenue in the Williamsburg section of Brooklyn. The fish monger was a short, round, dark-haired, dark-eyed Italian-American looking man, with a long, white, stained apron. He commanded the fish counter. You knew it was his domain by the way his elbows rested on the counter and by his booming voice. There was a long line, and we waited our turn. When it was our time to be helped, we ordered two pounds of baccala. The fish monger stared at us for a few seconds, then asked, "When are you planning to eat this?" knowing full well it was for the traditional Christmas Eve dinner. Jeremy replied, "Tomorrow." This one word set the fish monger into full swing. He started waving his arms in the air, shaking his head from side to side as if to say no, and then looking at us with disdain, he replied, "You can't. You're too late." He turned and glared at me with a look that said that I, being the mother, should have known better. Then he shot back, "You should have come to see me two days ago." Jeremy politely told him that we were going to give it a try.

The fish monger again replied, only this time in a louder voice, "You're too late. You can't. Why didn't you come in two days ago? I'm telling you, you can't do this." Then I spoke up, trying to diffuse the situation, by telling him that he was right, that ideally we should have come in two days ago, but we couldn't, and we still wanted the baccala. He just stood there shaking his head in disbelief. I was ready to walk out empty-handed because I could tell he was getting very agitated. Then, suddenly, he tore off a sheet of white waxed paper, reached into the barrel for the cod fish and started wrapping it up, the entire time shaking his head "no." He gave us our fish without a word, we paid for it, and as we were walking out the door, he called out reminding us, "You can't. You're too late."

As Jeremy and I were walking to the car, I remarked to Jeremy about how typical that exchange was with the fishmonger. It made me think about the unspoken Italian tradition of thinking that you can butt into anyone else's business and that was okay. It's as if, "your business is my business," and there is only one way of doing things, and that's my way.

On the way home, we talked about how that encounter made us feel. I admitted to Jeremy that I had feelings of not being a very good mother, waiting so late to buy the baccala. Jeremy admitted that he felt like he wasn't a very good son – that he "should have picked up the baccala long before I arrived." We ended up laughing over all these mixed up feelings, which are a testament to our Italian-American culture.

We soaked the cod fish for 24 hours, changing the water very often. Anxiety must have caused us to awaken to change the water during the night, since we didn't set an alarm clock. As it turned out, it worked, but I don't recommend having to interrupt sleep to make this delicious dish. Nor do I recommend tangling with a combative fish monger in order to do it. Ideally, soaking the salted cod fish for 48 hours and changing the water frequently is the way to go.

Scungelli Salad – Conch

My mother used canned conch for this dish. One year, we tried fresh conch and it turned out fine, but was a lot more work. Be mindful of the cooking time if you decide to use fresh conch because overcooking it even just a little bit makes it tough and rubbery.

Serves: 6–8

INGREDIENTS:

2 large cans of scungelli (29 ounces each)

⅓ cup olive oil – may need more

3–4 cloves garlic, chopped

½ cup Italian parsley, chopped

6 tablespoons fresh lemon juice plus lemon wedges

½ teaspoon salt

Fresh ground pepper, to taste

Dried red pepper flakes, to taste (optional)

METHOD:

Drain scungelli. Rinse well. Place scungelli in boiling water and cook for 1 minute. Drain and cool. Begin to add ingredients, tasting as you go along. Mix well, cover and refrigerate.

TO SERVE:

Approximately 30 minutes prior to serving remove from refrigerator. Serve on colorful platter and garnish with sliced lemon wedges.

Aunt Julia's Shrimp Scampi

Serves: 6–8 as a side dish

INGREDIENTS:

2 pounds shrimp, peeled and deveined

1 fresh lemon

4 cloves garlic, chopped

Olive oil

Handful Italian parsley, chopped

METHOD:

Sauté shrimp and garlic in olive oil. Place in baking dish, squeeze fresh lemon over shrimp and cover. Bake in 350° oven and let steam for 10 minutes or until shrimp are cooked. Uncover and let stand for a few minutes.

TO SERVE:

Sprinkle with chopped Italian parsley. Serve warm.

> *My uncle, Nicholas Castellano, was my father's oldest brother and was married to a beautiful woman, my Aunt Julia Ferrari Castellano. They had one daughter, Angela, who is about one year younger than I. Angela and I were and still are friends. Not only were we first cousins, but we shared the same names: Angela Michele Castellano and Michele Angela Castellano. As Lorrie mentioned, Aunt Julia was nothing less than gorgeous. Uncle Nick was quiet and reserved. Aunt Julia was lively, fun, and a joy to be around.*
>
> *Aunt Julia lived during a time when, unfortunately, there was not much treatment for breast cancer. When she was diagnosed there was little to be*

done, and she died in 1956 when she was 35 years of age. Her daughter, Angela, was 7 years old. It was such a great loss to all of us, but especially to Angela. After her mother died Angela spent just about every weekend at our house. Her father would drop her off on Friday afternoon after school and pick her up on Sunday afternoon. Angela and I were inseparable, and I have so many happy memories of our weekends together. Angela was crazy about my father, her Uncle Joe. They had a little routine that they did every Friday night. Right before my father came home from work, Angela would hide in the living room, usually behind a chair or sofa. When my father would walk through the door, he would say loud enough for her to hear, "She's not here, is she?" Of course, we all knew he was referring to Angela. I would tell him that she couldn't come this weekend. He then would say, "Good, I better look for her, just in case." He would then walk around the living room, checking behind the sofa and chairs and, predictably, would find her. He greeted her with, "What, you again?" And she would laugh and promise him that this was her last weekend to come to visit and they would then give each other a hug. For some reason, he affectionately called her "Cabbage Head," which she loved hearing because it made her laugh. They did that routine every Friday night for several years. My parents had a great love for Angela, and she felt the same towards them. Occasionally, I would go to her house on the weekends. Our grandma, Fanny Castellano, and our Aunt Dolly, Josephine Castellano Vuocolo, went to live with Uncle Nick and Angela after Aunt Julia died and they took care of both of them.

One time when Aunt Julia was still alive, I was visiting them. Aunt Julia was going shopping, and she left Angela and me under the care of their housekeeper. She promised she would bring something back for each of us. I was so excited about the prospect of Aunt Julia choosing a gift for me because, even at a young age, I knew her taste was extravagant. When she arrived home later that afternoon, sure enough she had a little bag for me and one for Angela. I don't remember what Angela got, but I do remember my surprise. When I opened it up, it was a small, boxy purse with a short strap, all of it covered in medium gray suede, with a large gold latch and gold closure on it. I had never owned something as beautiful or grown up as that. I kept that purse for many years and wish I still had it. The memory of it is very fresh in my mind and I can still picture it. Leave it to Aunt Julia – she didn't bring home a toy or a doll for her 7-year-old niece. Instead she chose a very elegant suede pocketbook with shiny gold trim.

My mother and Aunt Julia were friends, and my mother said Julia made the best shrimp scampi. My mother continued to make it after Aunt Julia died, but admitted that it wasn't as good as hers. I found this recipe in my mother's handwriting, labeled "Julia's Shrimp."

Shrimp & Roasted Peppers

Serves: 6 as a side dish

INGREDIENTS:

1 jar of roasted red peppers, or use fresh peppers and my mother's roasted peppers recipe in this book.

1 pound of medium shrimp, peeled and deveined, and boiled until they turn pink

2 tablespoons Italian parsley, chopped

2 tablespoons fresh mint, chopped, plus small amount for garnish

Juice of ½ fresh lemon, plus 1 lemon for garnish

Salt and pepper to taste

2 tablespoons olive oil

METHOD:

Combine all ingredients together in a large bowl. Mix well.

TO SERVE:

Place on shallow platter and set aside for about 30 minutes. Serve at room temperature.

Garnish with lemon wedges and fresh mint.

This recipe was created by my son, Jeremy, and daughter-in-law, Clare, on Christmas Eve, 2003. They were looking for a shrimp dish that was more colorful than regular scampi, and reflected the season. Using red roasted peppers and fresh green mint, it makes a beautiful presentation, is easy to prepare and is a very tasty dish. We have been making this every Christmas Eve since.

Fried Smelts

Serves: 6–8 as an appetizer and side dish

INGREDIENTS:

4 pounds of whole, fresh smelts

2 cups flour

Salt and pepper

Olive oil

METHOD:

Rinse, drain and pat dry smelts. Heat oil in frying pan or fryer. Oil is at the right temperature when you drop a pinch of flour in it and it sizzles. Place flour, salt and pepper in a paper or plastic bag. Place smelts in bag and shake, coating each one. Drop in fryer and cook until coating is golden brown.

TO SERVE:

Best served immediately. This is a great finger food while having your first Christmas Eve drink.

> This is one of the few fried foods I remember eating while growing up. Even as a child, I loved this salty, crispy little fish. My mother would fry these in a black iron skillet on her gas stove and they would come out light, crispy and golden. This is one of those dishes that she served immediately because she said the fish would get soggy if it sat too long. It almost never did because it was so delicious it was eaten up immediately.
>
> Today, when we prepare this dish for Christmas Eve, we use an electric fryer, a "Fry Daddy," and it does the trick! It's become a tradition to plug in the fryer outside, and stand around watching them cook while having a Christmas drink. We usually end up eating smelts as an appetizer because they are so tasty right out of the fryer.

Chapter 12

SWEETS
Dolci

Desserts of any kind, including cookies and soft drinks, were a very rare treat when we were growing up. Dessert after dinner was usually reserved for a holiday, or a special occasion, such as a birthday or when special guests were at our table. More often than not, there wasn't anything sweet to eat in the pantry. On the rare occasion when we did have cookies, my parents usually restricted it to one or two per person. Soft drinks were practically unheard of, except for holidays. It always surprised me when going to my friend's house on a Friday night for a sleepover and being offered orange soda and cookies for a snack.

At holidays my mother did a lot of baking which included cakes and cookies. Sometimes my parents' friends or other family members would bring a box of Italian pastries or Italian cookies when they came for dinner. Seeing that white, square cardboard box with the white string tied around it was always a happy sight. You could smell the powdered sugar before the box was even opened. Even then, my mother would restrict us by cutting the delicate pastries in half for each of us to have a taste.

Many of my mother's baking recipes are lost. A few survived. As we each grew up and left home, she baked less and less, and the recipes disappeared. Sweets, although we loved them, were not a big part of our lives. My mother was always health-conscious, making sure she gave us the freshest vegetables and fruits to eat. My mother knew what she was doing when she limited processed foods.

Aunt Josie's Sesame Cookies

Serves: makes about 40 cookies

INGREDIENTS:

4 cups all-purpose flour

1 teaspoon baking powder

Pinch of salt

1 cup sugar

2 sticks butter

1 tablespoon orange juice

2 teaspoons vanilla

3 eggs

¾ cup milk

½ pound sesame seeds

> Aunt Josie, Josephine Castellano, was my father's paternal aunt. I have a dim memory of Aunt Josie. Occasionally I would visit her with my Grandma Castellano, or she would come to our house in West Orange, New Jersey. When she visited, she usually brought these cookies. She was friendly, with a hearty laugh, and always elegantly dressed, complete with veiled hat, white gloves and black high heel shoes. My mother loved these cookies and baked them at holidays.

METHOD:

Soak sesame seeds in room-temperature water, then drain and spread out on a large plate. Blend sugar and butter. Add orange juice, vanilla and eggs. Beat together. Mix together dry ingredients. Blend dry and wet ingredients, alternating them, until dough ball is formed. Knead dough until ball is completely formed. Roll dough, forming a long "rope." Cut into 1½-inch pieces. Roll pieces in milk, then in sesame seeds. Chill 1 hour. Place on greased cookie sheet. Bake at 375° for 12 minutes or until sesame seeds look toasted.

TO SERVE:

Cool and place on a white paper doily on a colorful plate and serve.

When there was a large amount of baking to be done, such as a special occasion or holiday, Rosie Conforti and my mother would bake together. They had a nice synergy in the kitchen, whether they were canning tomatoes or baking cake. This is one of Rosie's favorites.

Rose Conforti's Pound Cake

Serves: 15

INGREDIENTS:

½ pound butter

2 cups sugar

4 eggs

2 cups milk

5 cups flour

1 teaspoon salt

5 teaspoons baking powder

1 tablespoon mace or ½ tablespoon nutmeg

2 teaspoons vanilla

METHOD:

Preheat oven to 350°. Grease and flour a tube pan. Using a mixer, cream the butter and sugar. While beating, add the eggs one at a time. Mix the flour, salt, baking powder and mace or nutmeg together in a separate bowl. Add the flour mixture and the milk, alternating the two. Mix in the vanilla. Pour into the tube pan and bake for 1½ hours or until a toothpick comes out clean. Cool in pan for 30 minutes, then remove and place on baking rack.

Icing

INGREDIENTS:

1 cup powdered sugar

¼ cup orange juice

Grated rind of one orange

METHOD:

Mix all ingredients until smooth and pour over cooled cake

TO SERVE:

This is a versatile pound cake. It can be toasted and buttered and served with afternoon coffee, or with ice cream for dessert. It lasts days in the refrigerator so it's great for unexpected visitors.

Mrs. Bromer's Coffee Cake

Serves: 15

INGREDIENTS:

2 packages yeast

1 cup water

1 cup sugar

6½ cups flour

4 eggs

1 teaspoon salt

1 cup milk

½ pound butter

2 teaspoons vanilla

METHOD:

Dissolve 2 packages of yeast in water. Add sugar, 6 cups flour, eggs, and salt and beat together. Scald 1 cup milk, add butter and vanilla. Mix all ingredients together, adding ½ cup flour at the end. Let rise in a warm location for 2 hours. Place in greased tube pan and bake 350° for 1 hour. Place on a cake rack and cool for 5 minutes, then remove from pan.

TO SERVE:

Can be served at room temperature, or toasted with butter and jam, and served with a cup of tea or coffee.

Mrs. Bromer was our neighbor in West Orange. She was from Germany and spoke English with a German accent. She and my mother were what I would call "neighbor friends." They weren't close, but they did share a love of food, and they often sent each other samples of what they had cooked or baked. Many times I would be the messenger, making deliveries between our houses. My mother usually made this coffee cake in the summer time at our house in Lake George, New York. As a way to pay the mortgage, my mother rented rooms in our little red cottage. Often times my sisters, brother and I would have to give up our bedrooms and sleep in the kitchen. My mother would make the cake the night before and serve it to the guests at breakfast. She set up cots in the kitchen and for most of the summer that is where we slept.

My brother Joe was a baby and still in a crib, and he slept in there with us too. Because the kitchen was small and we were packed in, his crib was usually pushed up against the kitchen counter, giving him easy access to the cake. In the early morning hours, his little hand would break through the aluminum foil covering the cake and he would reach in and take fistfuls of cake out and eat them. When my mother would discover it in the morning, she would be furious, but there wasn't much she could do about it then. This cake was often served to guests with little indentations in it – evidence that my baby brother had visited it in the night!

Aunt Lucy's Thumbprint Butter Cookies – *Marmellata Riempito Biscotti al Burro*

Lucy LaPlaca was Johnny San Giacomo's mother's sister. This recipe was one of Johnny's favorites. He always said, "You can't eat just one." When my mother made these cookies, my job was to make a thumb print in the cookie dough so she could fill it with jam.

Serves: about 24 cookies

INGREDIENTS:

½ pound butter, room temperature

½ cup sugar

2 egg yolks

1 teaspoon vanilla

2 cups flour

¾ cup raspberry jam

METHOD:

Cream together butter and sugar. Add yolks, vanilla and flour. This makes a sticky dough. Refrigerate for a few minutes or until it feels cold. Roll into small balls. Place on greased cookie sheet and make thumb impression on top of each cookie. Fill with raspberry jam. Bake at 350° for 10 minutes or until brown on bottom.

TO SERVE:

Place on colorful plate with a paper doily and enjoy.

Mary Jo's Cream Puffs – *Bocconcini con Crema*

Serves: 12 medium to large cream puffs

INGREDIENTS:

1 cup water

½ cup butter

¼ teaspoon salt

1 cup flour

4 large eggs

METHOD:

Heat water, butter and salt to a full rolling boil. Reduce heat and quickly stir in flour, mixing vigorously with wooden spoon until mixture leaves sides of pan in a

> *My sister, Mary Jo Castellano San Giacomo, is a lover of foods smooth and creamy. Although never being one who showed much interest in cooking, Mary Jo enjoys baking. This recipe, along with Aunt Lucy's Butter Cookies, are her favorites. Aunt Lucy was the aunt of Mary Jo's husband, John Thomas San Giacomo. Johnny passed away suddenly in 2005 and we miss him very much. Johnny was a great guy who laughed easily, loved to eat, and was a lot of fun. His greatest love, aside from Mary Jo, was his love of vintage cars, and he had plenty of them stashed all over Orange, New Jersey. When my father decided to finally part with his 1947 Chevrolet, he gave it to Johnny, who was then 16 years old. That was the beginning of his car tinkering and collecting. Johnny was an important part of our family for almost 50 years. As a young teen, he would hang around our house (he lived just a couple of blocks away) hoping to catch a glimpse of Mary Jo. He joined the U.S. Navy in the late 1950s and when he came home on leave, the first place he'd stop was our house so he could see her. He would walk down Rollinson Street, coming from the bus stop on Northfield Avenue in West Orange, New Jersey, dressed in his "blues" (blue sailor's uniform with long blue tie) and his white sailor's hat. He was a proud Navy seaman and carried that pride of serving in the U.S. Navy with him his entire life. Mary Jo knew that Johnny loved sweets, and she perfected this recipe just for him.*

ball. Remove from heat and beat in eggs one at a time, beating on low speed after each egg until mixture is smooth. Drop dough from stainless steel teaspoon onto greased cookie sheet, forming mounds three inches apart. Bake in preheated oven, 400°, for 10 minutes. Lower heat to 350° and bake for 25 minutes. Puffs are ready when doubled in size, golden brown and firm to the touch.

Remove from oven and cut the side of each with a sharp knife. Put the puffs back in turned-off oven for 10 minutes. Leave oven door open. Remove and cool puffs on rack and fill. Makes 12 large or 16 medium puffs. They freeze well without the filling for about two months.

Cream Filling

INGREDIENTS:

1½ cups milk	2 tablespoons cornstarch
½ cup heavy cream	2 tablespoons flour
¾ cup sugar	2 tablespoons butter
1 whole egg	1 teaspoon vanilla
2 egg yolks	Confectioner's sugar

METHOD:

Combine milk, cream, and 5 tablespoons sugar in saucepan; set aside. Whisk the whole egg, egg yolks, cornstarch, flour, and 2 tablespoons sugar. Bring milk mixture to a full boil. Pour half the milk mixture into egg mixture and whisk until smooth. Return this mixture to saucepan containing the rest of the milk. Stir over low heat until smooth and thick. Just when mixture begins to boil, remove from heat and stir in butter and vanilla.

Transfer to clean, dry bowl and cover with plastic wrap. Plastic wrap should rest directly on cream surface to prevent a skin from forming. (If you overcook cream, it will curdle. If it is lumpy, strain as you transfer it from pan to bowl). When cream has cooled, fill puffs and sprinkle with confectioner's (powdered) sugar. Refrigerate.

TO SERVE:

These look pretty served on a large glass plate covered with a paper doily.

MARY JO ADDS: It's easier to make them than to write the recipe!

Italian Cream Cake – *Torta alla Crema di Italiano*

Serves: 8

INGREDIENTS:

1 cup buttermilk

1 teaspoon baking soda

5 eggs, separated

2 cups sugar

1 stick butter

½ cup shortening

2 cups sifted all-purpose flour

1 teaspoon vanilla extract

1 cup pecans, chopped

1 cup coconut, shredded

METHOD:

Preheat oven to 325°. Combine baking soda and buttermilk and let stand a few minutes. Beat egg whites until stiff and set aside. Cream sugar, butter and shortening. Add egg yolks, one at a time, beating well after each addition. Add buttermilk alternately with flour to creamed mixture. Stir in vanilla. Fold in egg whites. Gently stir in pecans and coconut.

Bake in three greased and floured 9-inch round layer pans for 45 minutes or until cake tests done. Frost cooled cakes.

TO SERVE:

Place on cake plate on white paper doily and serve.

Cream Cheese Icing

INGREDIENTS:

1 package cream cheese (8 ounces), softened

1 stick butter, room temperature

1 pound confectioner's (powdered) sugar

1 teaspoon vanilla

METHOD:

Cream cheese and butter well and add vanilla. Beat in sugar a little at a time until of spreading consistency. Spread icing on cooled cake layers.

Mom with Michele's Italian Cream Cake

I showed my mother this recipe many years ago, after cutting it out of the Houston Chronicle newspaper. She was about to celebrate her 70th birthday, and I wanted to bake something special for her. When she read the recipe, she said, "This reminds me of the recipe your father's aunts used to use. It's authentic." She said it with such authority and approval, I decided to make it for her. After tasting it on her 70th birthday, she said it was so rich she only wanted it for special birthdays! So, I made it for her 80th and 90th birthdays too.

I never understood why she would limit or deprive herself of something as simple as a cake she enjoyed. Maybe it had something to do with Italian-American women and their inclination to "save" things that they loved. For example, my mother had beautiful hand towels that her mother had given her as a wedding present. They are from Italy and are made out of fine Italian linen. My mother saved them all those years and when I got married she gave them to me, telling me to "put them away and save them." Even though I have always used the pretty things I have, including using my sterling silver flatware every day all these years, I saved those towels. For many years, they were wrapped in tissue paper. A few years ago, I removed the tissue paper in which they were wrapped and placed them in my linen closet, and I still haven't used them!

Aunt Mena's Crostoli (Bow Knots)

Serves: makes about 25

INGREDIENTS:

3 eggs, lightly beaten

1½ tablespoons sugar

⅛ teaspoon salt

½ teaspoon almond extract

¼ teaspoon orange extract

1½ cups all purpose flour

1 tablespoon butter

1½ cups peanut oil

Confectioner's (powdered) sugar

METHOD:

Beat eggs lightly, add sugar, salt, almond extract and orange extract. Place flour on board, cut in butter, and add egg mixture. Knead until smooth. If too soft, add more flour. Roll thin and cut with pastry cutter into ¾-inch wide strips 6 inches long and tie into a bowknot. Fry in hot peanut oil until brown. Drain.

TO SERVE:

Sprinkle with confectioner's sugar and place on colorful plate.

> *Philomena Castellano Fried, my Aunt Mena, was my father's oldest sister. As Lorrie mentioned, she let us into her closet, drawers and jewelry box so we could play "dress-up." She had an elegant and sometimes exotic way of dressing. She was the only woman I knew who wore animal prints, mainly in sweaters, blouses and scarves. She had beautiful red hair, and it was always perfectly coiffed. She lived with us for a while. After she moved out on her own,*

when she came to visit she would always bring little presents, such as a small wrapped bouquet of Charms Lollipops.

My best memories of Aunt Mena involved going to her house on weekends. Before she married Uncle Bert, she lived in a beautiful, old, well-kept apartment building in Belleville, New Jersey. It was called an efficiency apartment – one big room, with a tiny kitchen hidden by an accordion door. There was a Murphy bed behind double solid oak doors. I was filled with excitement when Aunt Mena would open those big wooden doors and lower the bed. The apartment had floor to ceiling windows that let in a lot of light. Shortly after she moved in she made café curtains for those windows, which were very popular at that time. Only Aunt Mena did not use ordinary curtain fabric, she used pink thin-whaled corduroy! As a 9-year-old, I was enthralled with those curtains. During those special weekends with Aunt Mena, we would spend Saturdays doing "girl things." Aunt Mena taught me how to give myself a manicure and pedicure, how to brush my hair, how to care for my skin and clothes, and how to polish my shoes.

Our weekends began with my packing a bag, leaving home on Friday after school, and walking to the train station. I took the train from West Orange, New Jersey, to Newark, New Jersey, where Aunt Mena worked for the FHA (Federal Housing Administration). I loved going to her office, which was a huge place, with desks and people everywhere. She would take me around to introduce me to her co-workers. It was great fun and made me feel good because she was so proud of me. Then, we would leave, and go to the bus stop to catch the bus to her apartment. There was always a "pretzel man" on the corner near the bus stop, and she always bought a big, warm, salty, doughy pretzel for me, which was presented in a small brown paper bag. I munched on it while waiting for the bus.

Once the bus arrived in front of her apartment, we crossed the street to the small neighborhood grocery store and we picked out what we were going to eat for supper. And the biggest treat of all was that I could choose a comic book of my choice! I usually chose an "Archie and Veronica" comic book, and sometimes a coloring book with a new box of crayons.

While Aunt Mena cooked, I read my comic book and sometimes colored in the coloring book, or traced the images in the comic book and then colored them in. It all felt very peaceful, orderly and safe. Comparing it to the chaos of being at home with my parents, siblings, and the ever-present extended family, this was heaven to me. Aunt Mena's apartment was everything my home was not – quiet, neat, elegant – and being there with her had a huge impact on my life and in influencing who I became. She taught me the value of taking quiet time for myself and the value of taking good care of myself.

Although Aunt Mena cooked all our meals, I don't remember any special dish that she prepared. I do remember that she always set the table, and the two of us sat down together around her black wrought iron table with the pink Formica top and talked and ate. In later years, after she married Uncle Burt and moved to their house on the Metedeconk River in Bricktown, New Jersey, she cooked a lot of meat and potatoes dishes because that's what her husband liked.

She loved sweets, especially Italian cookies and pastries such as crostoli, and she usually had them on hand to serve them to family and friends.

Mom's Struffoli

Serves: Makes one small bowl

INGREDIENTS:

1 cup flour

2 eggs, beaten

¼ teaspoon salt

3 cups peanut oil for frying

METHOD:

Combine the flour and salt in a large bowl. Make a well in the middle and add the 2 eggs. Mix together and knead until the dough is smooth. Pinch off an egg-size piece of dough and with floured hands, roll it to form a rope about ¼-inch thick. Cut the rope into ¼-inch pieces. Repeat until all the dough is used. Keep your hands and the surface well floured to avoid sticking. In a deep skillet, heat the peanut oil. It is hot enough when a dough ball sizzles when it hits the oil and doesn't sink to the bottom. The secret of making good struffoli is very hot oil. Place the dough balls in the skillet, leaving enough room that they don't stick together. Take them out with a slotted spoon when they are golden brown on all sides, about 2 minutes. Repeat until all the dough balls are cooked, making sure the oil is hot enough for each batch. Place them on paper towels to drain excess oil.

Honey Coating

INGREDIENTS:

1 large jar honey

2 tablespoons tangerine peels, chopped or grated

2 tablespoons extra-dry vermouth

Colorful sprinkles

METHOD:

In a heavy pot large enough to hold all the dough balls, combine all ingredients except the sprinkles. Heat until when tested between thumb and finger, the honey sticks together slightly. Remove from heat and add the struffoli to the honey mixture, coating each dough ball.

TO SERVE:

Stack the dough balls into the shape of a pyramid and scatter with colorful sprinkles.

Struffoli was prepared every Christmas, and that is the only time I remember my mother making them. For many years, my mother served them in a green ceramic dish that was in the shape of a Christmas tree. If we visited relatives or friends of my parents, you could be certain there would be a small plate of struffoli offered to commemorate the Christmas holiday.

Rose Conforti's Knots – Italian Wedding Cookies

Serves: 10 dozen

INGREDIENTS:

5½ cups flour

½ teaspoon salt

1 tablespoon baking powder

¾ cup butter, softened

1½ cups sugar

4 eggs

½ cup milk

1 teaspoon orange or lemon zest

1 teaspoon lemon extract

1 teaspoon anise extract

METHOD:

Preheat oven to 350°. Grease two cookie sheets. In a bowl, combine the flour, salt and baking powder. Set aside. In a large bowl, cream the butter and sugar. Set aside. Beat the eggs with the milk, extracts and zest. Add the sugar and butter to the flour mixture and then slowly add the eggs. When the ingredients are moistened, turn out onto a floured board and knead for 2 or 3 minutes until the dough is smooth.

Wrap the dough in wax paper and refrigerate for an hour so that dough is easier to handle. Place the dough on a floured cutting board. Pinch off enough dough to make a rope about 6 or 7 inches long and as thick as your ring finger. Tie into a knot and place on greased cookie sheet. Bake 12 to 15 minutes or until very lightly browned.

Icing

INGREDIENTS:

2 cups powdered sugar

4 tablespoons whole milk (more if needed to thin icing)

¼ teaspoon almond extract

Colored sprinkles

METHOD:

Add all ingredients, except the sprinkles, in a bowl and mix until smooth. Dip the top of each cookie in the icing and let dry.

TO SERVE:

Place on a plate and arrange the cookies into a pyramid. Sprinkle the entire plate with colorful sprinkles.

LORRIE ADDS:

Knots always remind me of Italian weddings when I was growing up in the '40s. At my cousin Mary Ann Stefanelli Dinardo's wedding there was a gigantic platter of knots piled high that looked like a small mountain. Each cookie had a silver confection on it in the shape of a ball (called a dragee). I don't remember any wedding cookies at any wedding I've been to since, but I'll never forget that pile of Italian wedding cookies.

Pizzelle

Serves: makes about 12

INGREDIENTS:

⅓ cup heavy cream

1 cup plus 1 tablespoon all-purpose flour

½ cup sugar

⅓ cup whole milk

1 large egg

½ teaspoon anise extract

2½ tablespoons melted unsalted butter

METHOD:

Combine all ingredients and beat with mixer until smooth. Cover and refrigerate 1 hour. Preheat pizzelle iron and when ready, spray with nonstick, butter flavored cooking spray. Place a heaping tablespoon of the batter in the center of each form. Close the top of the pizzelle iron and squeeze the handles for about 30 to 40 seconds. The pizzelles should be golden brown – not dark brown. Using the edge of a small knife, carefully lift and peel each one out and place on a wire rack to cool. Repeat using the remaining batter. You may have to re-spray the iron in between. Cool pizzelles completely before serving or storing.

I loved it when my mother made these thin wafer cookies because not only were they delicious, they were so pretty to look at. In order to make these cookies, a pizzelle iron is needed. It is a small, heavy iron (much like a waffle iron), only the design it makes on the batter is a round, flower-like design. Usually, they are made for festivals, and a few years ago when I went to an Italian festival in Baltimore, the old Italian ladies in their long front aprons were lined up in front of their pizzelle irons making them and selling them. For years, my mother used that iron, and she always knew how long to keep the handles down so that the pizzelles came out a golden brown. I now wonder how she did that, and also wonder whatever happened to that old iron.

TO SERVE:

Sprinkle with confectioner's (powdered) sugar or serve plain. Either way, they're good.

Chapter 13

Putting It All Together

It was January when our mother died. During her memorial, the New Jersey winter howled outside. The snow cocooned and muffled the world around us. When the last mourners left, we huddled together around a table in the tiny restaurant in our Manahawkin hotel. We threw our coats off, welcoming the steamy heat of that cozy room and ordered a bottle of wine. We hadn't been together for quite some time since we'd arranged for one of us to visit our mother each month. Six of us at two times a year meant she had a visit from one of her children every month. Not much when you're growing old but, being spread far and wide over the country, it was the best we could do. Now on this cold January day, we were all together in her sleepy New Jersey town around the table once more.

We talked about and divided up the tasks that still needed to be done, thank you notes, bills to be paid. Wrapping up a life, especially a 96-year life, takes some doing, and we divided the tasks according to each siblings' strengths. Then we ordered dinner and enjoyed the comfort of one another. The rest of the family, spouses, children and grandchildren soon joined us. When the food was gone and the wine down to the last inch, we lingered as we always do, reluctant to leave. From the bar came guitar music and one of our favorite songs: Fly Me to the Moon. We literally danced to the bar and didn't stop till 3 a.m. Mom and Dad would have loved to see us having such a good time together. It was a celebration of their lives and the success of their parenting.

They'd set this scene for us through years of family gatherings, especially the gathering of the family around the dinner table every night. Those years of nightly dinners filled us with memories of the comfort and fun of sitting around a table together. And each of us has kept that tradition going. During those dinners they taught us to take care of each other and have fun together. And that's what we did on that cold January night in the small bar in Manahawkin, New Jersey, dancing and singing to the wee hours.

One of the ways my mother made things seem so effortless and enjoyable when we had a meal for six or 26 was her attention to the details of a well set table. She taught us that it doesn't have to be fancy, just functional. To her the food you served was only part of the equation.

One night I went to a friend's house for dinner. We were a group of women who knew and liked each other. We enjoyed long conversations over good food and wine. This night, the food was delicious, but I left feeling a sense of dissatisfaction. The conversation was choppy. The subject changed much too quickly. People seemed distracted. There was a lot of movement. The scene was not relaxed. I thought about what had happened, what had snatched from me the usual comfort of being with these wonderful friends. I gave it a lot of thought because I didn't want such a lost opportunity to happen again.

It was a simple answer: the table was not set in a way to encourage comfort and relaxation. Something was always missing. One of us was constantly getting up to get the serving spoon or the salt and pepper or a napkin. The food was on the table before all the chairs were found to accommodate everyone. The corkscrew could not be found. A well set table is easy to do and avoids all of this jumping up and down, leaving everyone with the feeling of vigilance. A relaxed attitude is impossible.

For my mother the answer was to have everything needed for that meal on the table before everyone sat down. That way everyone relaxes, unwinds and begins slowly to share the details of their day. There's something so comforting about sitting around a table with people you love. It's a way of connecting again, bringing their experiences and yours together. Even disagreeing is better done after a good meal and over a glass of wine or a bit of something sweet for dessert. When your table is comfortable, people tend to linger, and lingering strengthens relationships.

A dinner table is an anchor. It is the place to learn, to celebrate, to remember, to give and receive advice, compliments, to tell family stories. The food you serve is infused with family history. Everyone has a family history to pass on, and the dinner table is one of the best places to do it. So cook a good meal, set your table and invite the people you love.

Buon Appetito!

Child's place setting

Christmas table setting

Acknowledgments

Grazie to our brother, Joe Castellano, for advice and guidance about the publication process, for dropping everything and getting photos to us at the last minute, and for his detailed recipe on sausage making.

Thanks to brother-in-law and husband, Roger Fisher, for helping us through the maze of technology.

For contributing photos, thank you to our sister, Mary Jo San Giacomo, and our cousins, Roberta Hockin Lilley, Linda Castellano Koscielak, and Lucia Pellecchia Correll. Gratitude to our sister, Mena Castellano Scialli, for cooking and photographing her signature dishes.

To friend Bonnie Anderson, thank you for clarifying the many steps in the canning of tomatoes.

And a very hearty molto bene to our cousin, Angela Castellano Cosgrove, for cooking and photographing with enthusiasm on very short notice. It really helped us just when we needed it.

Many thanks to our daughter-in-law and niece, Clare Hilger, for saving the day by contributing additional much-needed photos.

Kudos to our son and nephew, Jeremy Jones, and to our daughter-in-law and niece, Clare Hilger, for proof reading.

Appreciation to Lynn Stegner at Stanford University who patiently read through the manuscript and gave innumerable and helpful suggestions.

Gratitude to the writer's group in Palo Alto, California, and to writing instructor Amanda Capps of Furman University in Greenville, South Carolina.

And thanks to all our family and friends who had to listen to us talk about this book for the last two years.

About the Authors

Michele Castellano Senac is a Registered Nurse and a contributing editor for *Natural Awakenings Magazine*. She was inspired to write *Around the Table,* her debut book, as a gift to her grown son to share timeless family recipes and the personal memories they evoked. She lives in South Carolina.

Lorrie Castellano, MA, LCSW is a psychotherapist, consultant and educator. *Around the Table* is her debut book, written out of love and appreciation for her immigrant grandparents and her desire to keep the roots of her family alive. She lives in California with her husband. She has two grown children and two grandchildren.

The authors are presently working on their second collaboration.

Michele Castellano Senac and Lorrie Castellano

Index

Antipasto 93
Arancini di Riso 100

Baccala 206
Bocconcini con Crema 222–223
Bow Knots 226
Braciole 110

Cake
  Coffee Cake 220
  Cream Cheese Icing 225
  Italian Cream Cake 224–225
  Pound Cake 219
Canning Tomatoes 167–174
  Lorrie's Canned Tomatoes 171–174
  Mom's Canned Tomatoes 171
Cappellini e Acciughe 204
Carciofi Ripieni 97
Castellano Family 31–54
  Josephine "Dolly" Castellano Vuocolo 49–53
  Joseph "Joe" John Castellano 72–82
  Loretta "Cleo" Cibella Castellano 56–71
  Michael Angelo Castellano 33–35
  Michael Angelo Castellano, Jr. 46–49
  Nicholas Ilaria Castellano 40–43
  Philomena "Fanny" Ilaria Castellano 36–40
  Philomena "Mena" Volpe Castellano Fried 44–45
Ceci e Pasta 137
Chicken and Potatoes 193
Christmas Eve 197–214
  Menu 201
Ciambotta 183
Cibella Family 3–30
  Angelina "Angie" Cibella Aulisi 19–20
  Camille Salvatoriello Cibella 8
  Eleanore Cibella Hockin 22–30
  Loretta "Cleo" Cibella Castellano 56–71
  Mary Cibella Stefanelli 16–18
  Rose Cibella 9–15
  Tomaso Cibella 8
Cod Fish, Salted 206
Conch 208

Cookies
  Italian Wedding 231–232
  Pizzelle 233
  Sesame Cookies 217
  Thumbprint Butter 221
Cream Puffs 222–223
Crostoli 226

Desserts 215–234
Dolci 215–234

Eggplant Parmigiana 179
Escarole and Beans 180–181
Everyday Meals 175–195

Feast of the Seven Fishes 197–214
Fennel and Olives 99

Garlic, Roasted 153

Insalata
  Caprese 103
  di Broccoli 152
  di Cime di Rapa 151
  di Natale 158
  di Pomodoro 156
  di Potate 154
  Finocchio e Olive 99
  Foglia 149
Italian dialect 71
Italian Sausage 115–117

Jambota 183
Jambought 183

LaFest' 78
Lasagna di Carnevale 142–143
Lentil Soup 177
Linguini e vongole 122

Marinara Sauce 113
Marmellata Riempito Biscotti al Bur 221
Meatballs 108–109

Meatless Tomato Sauce 113
Meatloaf 190
Menest' and Beans 180–181
Migliacchio 176
Minestra 180–181
Mozzarella and Tomatoes 103
Mushrooms, stuffed 90

Olive Oil 104

Parmigiana di Melanzane 179
Pasta 120
  Bows with Pot Cheese 140–141
  Cappellini & Anchovies 204
  Cavatelli 126–127
  Chickpeas and Pasta 137
  Farfalle alla Ricotta 140–141
  Fusilli, Ziti or Cavatelli with Broccoli or
      Cauliflower 132–133
  Ladies of the Night 138
  Lasagna 142–143
  Linguini and Clams 122
  Pasta alla Puttanesca 138
  Pasta con Pomodoro 114
  Pasta e Fagioli 135, 136
  Pasta 'Fazool' 136
  Pastina with 'the' Egg 129
  Peas and Pasta 130
  Ravioli 144–145
  Spaghetti with Olive Oil 124
Peperoni Arrostiti 94–95
Peppers
  Peppers and Eggs 186–187
  Roasted Peppers 94–95
  Sausage and Peppers 189
  Shrimp and Roasted Peppers 212
  Stuffed Hot Cherry Peppers 89
Piselli e Pasta 130
Pizza
  Anchovy Pizza 202
  Lorrie's Pizza 164–165
  Mom's Pizza 160–161
  Pizza con de Acciughe 202

Pizzelle 233
Polenta, Mom's 176
Polpette alla Napoletana 108–109

Quick Fresh Tomato Sauce 114

Ravioli alla Napoletana 144–145
Rice Balls 100

Salads
  Broccoli Rabe 151
  Broccoli Salad 152
  Christmas Day Salad 158
  Fennel and Olives 99
  Leafy Green 149
  Potato Salad 154
  Scungelli 208
  Tomato Salad 156
Salsa di Pomodoro con Salsiccia 111
Salsiccia Italiano 115–117
Sausage and Peppers 189
Scungelli 208
Setting the Scene 235–239
Shrimp and Roasted Peppers 212
Shrimp Scampi 210
Smelts, Fried 214
Spaghetti Aglio e olio 124
Spinach and Potatoes 184
String Beans and Potatoes 185
Struffoli 228–229
Stuffed Artichokes 97
Stuffed Rolled Steak 110
Sweets 215–234

Taralles 101
Tomatoes 107
  Canning Tomatoes 167–174
Tomato Sauce with Meat 106–107
Tomato Sauce with Sausage 111
Torta alla Crema di Italiano 224–225

Veal Cutlets 194

Made in the USA
Middletown, DE
24 November 2014